Capt'n Bob's Adventures *in* Child Psychology

ROBERT BELENKY

ISBN: 978-1-4834-2657-0 (sc)
ISBN: 978-1-4834-2656-3 (e)

Lulu Publishing Services rev. date: 02/20/2015

Dedication

To my ancestors

And my descendants ... Oliver, Alice, Michael,
Simon, Max, Ella and Sofia

And to all children, sad or happy, wherever they may live

And mostly to Mary.

http://www.robertbelenky.com/

Be your own educator, not the student of Paolo Friere.

—Paolo Friere

Contents

I

Antecedents

Grandma Jenny

Last night I dreamed that I was on a BMT subway train off to visit my mother. Her name was Sophie. She is lonely since my father died. I have not seen her in a long time. Too long. I am a negligent son, shall I say a bad son? On my lap I held a Mason jar full of jellied chicken soup wrapped awkwardly in a brown paper bag.

It was so many years ago that my mother and I sat on that same BMT train as it rattled under the Lower East Side. We were off to visit Grandma Jenny ("*Zhenya*" in Russian), a well-rounded, excessively social woman who at the end of her days lived alone in a dark apartment at 221 East Broadway. Her husband eighteen years her senior, Grandpa Mikhail ("*Mikhel*"), died when I was four. I remember him dimly but was never really close. He was a private, thoughtful man, shy, perhaps withdrawn, sentimental; an intellectual, a junkman who traded scrap metal while wending his way through the streets of New York's Lower East Side seated on a wagon that was drawn by a horse.

Grandpa Mikhel was sickly pale. He lay on a high bed in a dark room. His dirty yellow-gray mustache drooped to the sides of his mouth. The narrow, darkened chamber reeked sharp stinky. Pipe smoke? Medicine? Sweat? Old man's pee?

Grandpa Mikhel kissed me gently on the forehead. The pin pricks of his dirty yellow-gray mustache made me shiver. A black and gold oval-framed photograph revealing two people from a strange and

1

ancient world was mounted on the wall above him. "His parents," my mother explained.

Grandpa Mikhel's father's name was *"Lezamaycha"* from which my middle name, Louis, was derived.

Why did I call him "Grandpa" and not *"Zayda"* as one does in Yiddish? Maybe the reason is that Grandpa Mikhel was pleased leave the *shetl* (Jewish village) just south of St. Petersburg far behind and to become a real American.

He was Mikhail Gershewitz in Russia and Michael Mitchell here—his own idea, not the whim of an immigration officer. He was proud to have mastered the new culture and its language. He spoke only in English although he must have been entirely comfortable in both Yiddish and Russian. He spoke English whenever possible. My mother showed me a letter that he sent her on the occasion of her marriage to my father. It was well written but a bit on the flowery side by today's standards.

A distinctly Jewish neighborhood, Seward Park was packed with pushcarts. Grandma Jenny hauled me by the hand. We threaded the intemperate, impatient, cacophonous crowds. Grandma Jenny haggled over potatoes and bagels and cabbage and cucumbers and pickles; a squawking chicken. She traded strange words and ringing laughter with women in head scarves and men dressed in black. Back at the apartment, she told my mother that the man who sold her the chicken has a boy, "Smart? He could go to college. So smart. A doctor he should be."

Mom, you make me sick, my mother said. You are a gossip. You are immature. You mind everybody's business but your own. Your heart is no good. Your legs are swollen. You are out of breath. Why do you run to the market all the time? You are killing yourself.

In my dream I sat on the rattan seat of the BMT subway car. I was alone. Where was my mother? She needs me. She is lonely. She died twenty-three years ago. I have not seen her. I am not much of a son. She was a good mother but not a great daughter. Grandma Jenny was a gossip. Not malicious. The opposite. She knew everybody's business but her own. Why did she marry a man so old? Eighteen years, I think. Twenty maybe.

Grandma Jenny was sixteen or was it eighteen when they married. He was over forty. She was pretty but not when I knew her. She was fat. Old. Over sixty. Grandma and grandpa were cousins. First cousins. That is why, my mother explained, your uncles, Nathan and Arthur, have bad hearing. Genetics.

Grandma's older sister, *Tanta* (aunt) Lizzie, whom I never met was engaged to grandpa first. She was his intended. But somehow Grandma Jenny, who was prettier and not in the least restrained, beat her out. Tanta Lizzie never forgave her.

Grandma and grandpa didn't have much in common. Grandma was gregarious. She knew everybody's business but her own. She didn't care about religion one way or the other. Grandpa, the junkman, was an intellectual, an atheist. "Do you believe in God?" he was asked. "The more important question," he answered, "is— 'Does God believe in me?'"

Grandpa Mikhel played chess with a black man, his best friend. Imagine that, a black best friend in those days—on the East Side!

Grandpa Mikhel loved opera. He stood in the balcony at the Met where tickets were cheap. He knew every note. If the orchestra left out even one or played it wrong, he told everybody when he got home.

My mother thought that she and Grandpa Mikhel were similar, heady, self contained. Same with Uncle Arthur, her youngest brother who became an economist, a professor. She was made to watch his baby carriage when she wanted to play with her friends. One time it rolled down the cellar stairs. It was her fault. Uncle Ben was smart but undisciplined. At least he earned a living. Who knows what he would have done in another place and time? Uncle Nathan, a sentimental fur worker, a union man, a communist, a sports fan who loved Joe Louis, had a good mind but who knew it? He had bad hearing.

My mother married Max, my father, right after his third trip to Russia because he was a relatively uncomplicated man of action.

★★★★

Last week, we visited our son, Michael, his wife and two daughters, Sofia and Ella. Our dog, Jenny, was sprawled asleep on their floor. Sofia said, "I am grateful for our family because we love each other."

"It has been that way for generations," I said.

Cousin Boris

I shall now introduce my grandchildren to their ancestors. No time to waste. I am old. Who can say how long I have? Nobody has an interest in ancestor worship in our family. But maybe they should because—please note: There were people who walked the earth like giants and provided some of our progeny's DNA. Surely today's kids will find them worth knowing if given the chance.

Cousin Boris Holmstock, *"Golomschtock"* in Russian, was a good example. He was my father's first cousin, making him first cousin-once-removed to me. Boris was an excruciatingly funny man, an irrepressible clown, a man of the theater—the Second Avenue Yiddish Theater; yes: theatrical he was, larger than life.

I am not sure exactly what he did for work. I do know that he wrote at least one play. I stumbled upon it a few years ago in a secondhand book store on 4th Avenue. It was full of dumb, vaudeville humor, and superficial bawdiness. I recall that he also wrote reviews of plays for Yiddish newspapers of the time, probably the Socialist *Arbeit*. Who knows? He may have written for the more moderate *Forwartz* as well. His pen-name was "Ben Rhoda."

I also remember that he never had any money or maybe he lavishly spent what came his way. I know for certain that he was normally broke because I saw with my own eyes that he was always borrowing from my parents who considered him a pest, a moocher and less, far less, amusing than I did, a *"schnorer."*

Who is to say? I don't know. I don't remember. I am piecing stories together from fragments in my mind, words I heard that eluded comprehension. Boris never married. Aunt Selma said he was gay. And why not? He was certainly jolly. But who can ever know such things at such a distance?

Did Boris have a Yiddish accent? A Russian accent? He probably had a bit of each but whatever he had, I didn't hear it. I couldn't hear my father's accent. Everybody had an accent in those days.

Boris owned a racing bicycle. I had never seen one before. I was seven years old and much impressed. He would wrap a handkerchief over his head, tie a knot at each corner, roll up his pant legs, sing a silly song, hop on and race off to the post office to get the mail.

That was at our summer home, a little house on an acre of land in Brentwood, Long Island. My parents bought it for what? $1800? .... back in 1932 or 1933. A rusting Model A Ford sat incapacitated in the back yard. I, behind the steering wheel, went, *"Rrrrrr! Rrrrrr!"*

Boris was very handy. Maybe that's why my parents tolerated him. Without checking with them, he would march off to Lordan's Lumber Yard down the street, buy a truckload of wood along with tools and nails, charge the lot to my father's account, and proceed to build things. He built me a play house. A real house. But tiny. It had a downstairs with chairs and a table, kid sized, and an upstairs that was really an attic. There was even a little upstairs veranda. And it had two doors and a few screened windows. I don't remember how many. No lights, electricity or plumbing. He called it, "Bobby's Rest." I was "Bobby" in those days.

At first I played there with my friends but it was too small for much except sitting so mostly we played outside. Even though I gradually stopped using it, I loved having a house of my own.

Boris was a very funny man. He came downstairs in the main house one morning to join us for breakfast. We sat on the back porch at the long, wooden table that Boris had made for us, eating our pancakes. Boris danced in, shirtless, pant legs rolled up. He wore a white handkerchief on his head knotted at four corners and taped a wilted Blackeyed Susan to his chest. He called it a "Cockeyed Susannah,"

("Cockeyed Susannah!" I thought. That is the *funniest* name in the *world!*")

He sang a song with words like "*Deedle deedle, deedle.*"

I cracked up. I laughed so hard that I choked on my pancakes. My mother said, "Enough, Boris, already." My father said, "*Bariya!* Let him alone. The boy has to *eat!*"

That was not the worst harm Boris was capable of. When I was five, I spent a long time … a day and a night probably… in the hospital getting my tonsils out. I woke up groggy, my throat hurting so bad I can feel it now almost eighty years later. My mother fed me vanilla ice cream with a wooden spoon from a Dixie Cup.

That helped a little.

Boris showed up wearing a silly hat. "*Bobbila!*" he shouted. "I am *here!*" He sang a very funny song and danced an incomparably hilarious dance. I laughed. It hurt when I laughed but I couldn't stop. I laughed and laughed and laughed. I laughed so hard that I was not able to beg Boris to stop. "Please stop, Cousin Boris!" I wanted to yell. "*Please stop!*" But I was laughing so hard and hurting so bad that I could not say anything.

Sixty-five years later, we named our third dog, Boris.

Aunt Selma

Uncle Allen was the youngest of five brothers, eight years my father's junior. Born like the others in Smolensk, Russia, he was only seven when the family emigrated to America. He therefore learned to speak English with no discernible accent and became the most American of the five. Allen projected a princely elegance, the very embodiment of New York chic. He became a physician, first an eye, ear, nose and throat specialist with an office on fashionable Central Park South and later a psychiatrist. A longtime bachelor with a history of being seen with gorgeous girlfriends, he surprised the family by announcing that he had actually married one, a brilliant and beautiful young woman ... name of Selma.

Selma was introduced to us at Grandma Tamara's house in the Bronx. Grandma Tamara was Uncle Allen's mother. I was thirteen, in full puberty and therefore vulnerable. The lady blew me away. She was not only attractive in outward appearance but she had an easy, raucous laugh, was replete with funny stories and unlike most grownups actually showed an interest in us, the kids, cousins Peter and David, and me. I could tell right away that she and Uncle Allen were in love and I cheered them on.

Oh, Selma was cool all right, very cool. She knew everybody in the great world. She referred to Howard Fast as "Howie" and to Leonard Bernstein as "Lenny" as in, "Lenny told the funniest story last night at the party."

Married into the European generation of the family, Selma, although born in Montreal, grew up in Ohio and was a real American. She was optimistic, warm, witty and able to speak authoritatively about anything. She also swam, excelled in tennis, sang and played the piano. A phenomenon. What couldn't she do? Who and what didn't she know?

An example of Aunt Selma bridging cultures:

Grandma Tamara (speaking in Yiddish): "So, my son, Allen who is your husband, has become a psychiatrist. Tell me, Selma dear, what exactly *is* a psychiatrist?"

Aunt Selma: "A psychiatrist is someone who listens to a person's problems and helps them do the right thing."

Grandma: "Oh, yes. I understand: A psychiatrist is like a rabbi."

Selma herself became a psychoanalyst and no doubt a very good one but, I suspect, more prone to offering commanding advice than most.

"Aunt Selma," I said. "I am about to graduate college with a major in English and have no idea what to do for work."

"Become a psychologist," she instructed without hesitation.

Naturally, I followed her advice and never regretted it.

The culmination of Aunt Selma's life was Katrin's birth, the long-awaited princess who was everything her parents wished for: cute, clever, and fun. I visited the family at their summer cottage on Long Island. What a beautiful baby! What happy parents!

And so time went by. Katrin turned out to be just as marvelous as her mom and dad hoped she would be. But, sadly, her parents' marriage dissolved. Allen died soon after that. A catastrophe.

But life went on as one hopes it will and, with luck, sometimes does.

Eventually, Selma, newcomer to the Tamara matriarchy, became a matriarch of her own and will surely be remembered in family folklore as an elegant lady of brilliance, kindness and humor.

Jewish Collectives

Two thousand eleven: This is the year of life on the threshold of extreme old age, the start of my ninth decade. I will have lived four score years this summer come August.

How is such a thing possible? With advanced age comes disability in various forms, some odder than others. In my case, it is two-fold:

On the one hand, I am physically—although not yet (entirely) mentally—impotent. This is the result of a bilateral prostatectomy almost fourteen years ago in which the nerves on both sides of my body, those that lead to the control of erections, were unceremoniously snipped.

This means that I can no longer screw properly, a small sacrifice, I believe, for the privilege of remaining on earth. On the other hand, I can still walk, talk, eat, run, dance and enjoy the company of others even that of beautiful woman.

It is only a matter of screwing. There are benefits: a) I am still alive and b) (if I were not before) a perfectly safe companion. Some might consider the latter an insult, some a plus of sorts. Finally c) a minor disability makes me one of the crowd here in our retirement community, a *bona fide* citizen.

Mary doesn't seem to mind. She may well be relieved. As for me, I find myself, while still entertaining occasional libidinous thoughts, to be on the whole less distractible, more able to enter the world fully and with less blur than previously.

On the other hand, I am developing other, perhaps more disturbing signs of senescence about which one does not normally make a big deal.

For example, I am becoming sentimental about my legacy. I have taken to writing memoirs. I think about those who have come before me. I have read something of the history of Jews in Europe, about the Holocaust, but even more intriguing has been an escalating passion for information about the Jewish settlement and collective farm movements in Ukraine during the 1920s and 1930s.

I am in fact planning a visit to Ukraine in mid April [2011]. The purpose is to interview survivors of that remarkable episode in Russian/Jewish history. It is of interest to me in part because my father, Max, played an significant role in that movement and in part because the settlers for the most part were not Zionists but rather one brand of socialist or another, more acceptable traditions in my view.

The socialism of that time and place was often of a revolutionary yet humanistic sort exemplified by Russia's Jewish Bund party. Sure, some were Bolsheviks (Majority) and some were Zionists. But most were Menshevik (Minority) socialist-humanists, a felicitous species with which I readily identify.

Although a proud leftist all my life, I have never been much into Stalinism and indeed have come over the years increasingly to despise it. As for Zionism, it has always left me cold except for the early days after Israel's founding when the enterprise appeared heroic. Now, because of the Occupation of Gaza and the West Bank, it has become toxic, shameful and a betrayal of the decency that I had always imagined was integral to the Jewish tradition.

★★★★

The drumbeat has begun. I will be in Crimea in less than a week. My mind is aslosh with images of Simferopol, that far-away little city often confused in the minds of Americans with Sevastopol. Mary and I visited there four years ago to dip our toes in the waters of history, that terrible history of the area east of Poland and west of the Dnieper River so vividly described in *"Bloodlands,"* a book by Timothy Snyder that I recently read. It was there at the epicenter of anti Semitism that an alternative to the Zionist narrative was written.

But it was not only Jews who perished during the first half of the twentieth century. First it was the Ukrainians having been subjected to Stalin's manufactured famine of the early 1930s, the largest in the history of mankind prior to Mao's infamous repetition of the event some thirty years later on an even grander scale.

Who is to say? The people actually to suffer most prior to World War II may well have been Ukrainian ethnic Poles, long-time residents of the area and largely well assimilated.

And one should not forget Tartars, descendants of the mighty Genghis Khan, who Stalin left to die on Russia's frozen Steppes.

Regardless of ethnicity and despite their differences, great numbers perished in Ukraine at the hands of the Soviets and again by the Nazi invaders and their local acolytes. Countless numbers were shot, imprisoned, or banished to the cold horizons of Siberia.

My interest goes back before that. The story begins before my birth. My father, Max—Maksim Davidovich—Belenky was, like his four brothers, born in Smolensk, the great medieval city in western Russia on the eastern border of Belarus. The family was Jewish and Smolensk was beyond the pale of settlement but the Belenkys were permitted to settle because Max's father, my grandfather, David, was a watchmaker and his skills were useful to the Russians.

Thus by virtue of Grandpa David's trade and the good graces of Tsar Nikolai II, the family was raised in Smolensk. My grandma, Tamara, supplemented their modest income by preparing and selling take-out lunches to local Russian workers.

Like many Jewish boys at the time, Max dreamed of working the land. Both the Jews of the time and the anti-semites characterized Jews as *"luftmenschen,"* air people—"air heads" in US slang—because according to law and stereotype they did not work with their hands.

Many were in fact workers but except for the Jewish agricultural colony in Kherson created under an ukase by Tsar Alexander I, Jews were forbidden to own land; thus was farming for the most part closed to Jews. However, as it often happens, the more unlikely its realization, the more attractive a goal it became.

Most Jews, then, were reduced to work with their minds instead of their hands. To the extent that they were able to receive a formal education, they became lawyers and accountants, teachers and writers; merchants, money-lenders, rabbis and scholars. Seventy percent of shetl residents were small-time traders.

Agriculture in the shetl was reduced to puttering with window boxes, the labor of the dispossessed not of those who owned their destinies. Even under the Soviets, although anti-semitism was officially outlawed, Jews were pushed to society's margins. It was only industrial workers, peasants and soldiers, who were given full privileges of citizenship. Jews were none of these.

Thus it was the work of citizens—if not to say patriots—that attracted the Jewish youth, male and female, of the time; work with a tangible end product, work that led to the creation of a new and better society, work consistent with the socialist ideal; honest work marked by calloused hands, work on the horizons of possibility opened up first by the 1905 revolution with its slogans of equality echoing the American and French revolutions before it.

It was therefore not surprising that Max wanted to be a farmer. His oldest brother, Harry, a socialist in youth but a Zionist in old age, somehow managed to emigrate to America, the first in the family to do so. Max and his next older brother, Saul, followed in 1911. I am not sure why exactly they came. They were not particularly oppressed in Smolensk nor were they starving.

I suspect that adventure was the motive. They also wanted to visit a half sister whose name I have forgotten, a woman who emigrated with her mother, the first wife of Grandpa David (*"Dovid,"*), to Iowa. I remember that she once visited us in New York when I was little but, beyond being told that she was grandpa's only daughter—but not grandma's—I recall no details.

The first thing that Max and Saul did upon arriving in the Land of the Free was to hitch-hike to Iowa—not knowing a word of English—to see their half-sister.

The second thing that Max did was to enroll in the Baron de Hirsch Agricultural School in Peekskill, New York, with an affiliated campus in Woodbine, New Jersey. The mission of the school, financed by the Baron de Hirsch Foundation, was to train immigrant Jewish boys to become farmers. Max loved the place. We have a picture of him in our family album, a broad smile on his face, a sweat handkerchief on his head knotted at each of its four corners, milking by hand a most placid and delighted cow.

Upon graduation, Max, remembering his adventures in the American West and now having a better command of the English language, managed to get himself enrolled in the Michigan State Agricultural College located in Lansing. There he studied farm machinery and became a certified tractor expert.

Meanwhile, his mother and father, Grandma Tamara and Grandpa Dovid, a kindly man whom I barely remember, followed their three oldest sons, Harry, Saul and Max to America. They brought with them their two youngest sons, my uncles Jack and Allen.

The family first settled on the Lower East Side, then moved to Brooklyn; finally and more permanently, they came to the Bronx on 171st Street just a block from the Grand Concourse, the Champs Elysée of New York's immigrant Jews.

Meanwhile, big events were unfolding in Russia, the October Revolution for one. Jews, despite popular attraction to a moderate, democratic form of socialism, cheered—especially when it was declared that anti-Semitism was outlawed.

Optimism reigned.

But Soviet Russia was faced with apparently insoluble problems. One of these was a pervasive lawlessness so severe that it included a raging civil war, pogroms and rampant starvation. How to feed its people—including an army comprised largely of peasants? Who was left to farm the land?

Ukraine, once "Europe's Breadbasket," was now no longer able to feed itself. Famine followed famine. Cannibalism appeared.

Yet land there was in apparent abundance because the Soviet government had confiscated the great feudal estates.

Enter Herbert Hoover heading the "American Relief Administration," the ARA. The ARA was comprised of several Non Governmental Organizations among them the Friends' Service Committee and The JDC—the American-Soviet Jewish Joint Distribution Committee, "The Joint" in English and "*Dzoint*" in Russian.

The goal was to save Russia from itself. The ARA with its fiscal power won the reluctant support of the Lenin administration. But the Joint was welcomed warmly by Soviet Jews and tolerance mixed with concern by Ukrainian peasants.

The JDC, with funding largely from philanthropist Maurice Baron de Hirsch, in turn formed "Agro-Joint," the organization devoted to the support of Jewish agriculture in the Soviet Union.

Lenin saw the wisdom of solving the age-old "Jewish Problem" by encouraging the proletarianization of shetl Jews. The idea was to end their destiny as "*luftmenschen*" and to create a new culture built on the premise that a full member of society must be one who works on tangible objects, whether greenery or machinery.

That was just fine with young Jews like Max whose life goals were similar to those then in demand. No more trading; no more "exploiting others" through money-lending; no more withdrawal into books. What mattered now was to produce food for the benefit of the new socialist state and *all* of its citizens. Jews would lead the way.

From the shetls in the Pale and those cities beyond where some few of their number had been allowed to settle—as had Max and his family—came idealistic young people, probably much like the hippies who flocked to northern New England.

They arrived on the land that was offered to them in Crimea—including southern and central Ukraine—land for the most part snatched from the estates of aristocrats.

Much of it, in fact, was in the vicinity of settlements near the city of Kherson where, with the blessings of Tsar Alexander I, some Jews had been settled a century before; and not far from where Catherine the Great had placed Jews even earlier. Sending Jews to the South, an ambivalent attempt to solve Russia's perpetual "Jewish Problem," was not a new strategy.

At first these were simply agricultural endeavors but soon they became known as "collective farms" or, in a Russian neologism, "*kholkhozi.*"

The Soviet government was intent on collectivizing the farms of all Ukrainian peasants including Tartars and those of Polish, German, Hungarian and Bulgarian descent. But resistance within the non-Jewish farm population in Ukraine was very strong. Besides, there was no tradition anywhere for organizing agriculture on an industrial scale, something that required skill in invention, planning and bureaucracy.

Peasants knew how to farm, inefficiently perhaps but they had calloused hands and muscular arms.

Jews by contrast were small town and urban people. They had soft hands but they often had skills required for the operation of any organization.

Lenin figured that Jews would somehow help get the peasants collectivized by showing them how to run a collective farm as a business. The Jews in turn longed to farm but lacked the skills.

And ... there was Max Belenky in New York City, a native Russian and Yiddish speaker with a high level of certified training in modern agriculture; a tractor expert no less. Just the man needed.

Max was forthwith hired by the Joint Distribution Committee to return to Russia to introduce tractors to the newly arrived Jewish farm population. He became head of one of ten "tractor teams" with funding and machinery provided by the John Deere company.

He made three visits to Russia in that capacity, each lasting the greater part of a year. I am not sure of the dates. The first, I believe, was in 1922, the second in 1924, and the third in 1926.

The settlements, Jewish kholkhozi, were remarkably successful. Despite phenomenally difficult times, they prospered, indeed became models for the non-Jewish farms in the area with which they tended to work in a collaborative, mutually respectful manner.

Then Lenin died and Stalin emerged as head of state. Stalin's murderous enmity to Agro Joint was aroused by its support by Americans. "Spies!" he reasoned. "Capitalists!" "Jews!" He accused the leadership of treason and summarily executed most of them. Then came the Nazi catastrophe.

Some few Jews survived by escaping to the East just ahead of the Nazi invasion. After the war these people returned to Ukraine. Some are still alive. In the weeks to follow I shall interview as many of them as I can find.[1]

I can't wait.

---

[1] Reported in my book, "Collective Memories," Maddoggerel Publications, 2012

II

Formation

Funnies

During the summers in Brentwood, Long Island, the years that encompassed the Great Terror, the Hitler-Stalin Pact, Operation Barbarossa, Pearl Harbor, World War II and the Holocaust, Alan Ascher and I managed to get to Jones Beach two or three times a week. Our parents pooled their gasoline ration cards. That was sufficient to fill the tank of the Ascher's 1942 Cadillac as often as we had an urge for a dip in the ocean. Alan was my only friend during those Halcyon summers. Alan was cool. He knew all about boats, for example, but best of all, he was very entrepreneurial.

When we weren't bodysurfing the breakers into shore, we hiked up and down the beach, paper bags in hand. We were looking for empty soda bottles that would bring us two cents apiece in deposit money. For every five bottles—ten cents—we could buy a comic book. We developed quite a collection. It would be worth a lot of money today: the original Captain Marvel, first edition Batman, and early Katzenjammer Kids.

Blond Braids

He was fourteen, a skinny, average kid, neither a loner nor particularly gregarious nor was he morose although perhaps he sometimes came across as a bit preoccupied.

He thought about girls a lot, probably too much, and actually went out with one the year before at summer camp and once at a party in his friend's house experienced a startlingly pleasurable moment while hugging and kissing her in the dark.

But it got worse. Thoughts of girls intruded everything, distracted him uninvited. They had a life of their own.

Once in school while absorbed in a particularly difficult math test, his anxiety was somehow transformed into an autonomic sexual response; then, despite himself and much to his embarrassment, he became tumescent and ejaculated.

"How could that have happened?" he asked himself. "I was thinking about algebra, not girls."

He masturbated a lot, probably no more than other boys, but he became acutely aware of how much he was in the power of alien and inexplicable forces. It was this helplessness that worried him more than the urges themselves.

He was brought up in an agnostic home. Questions of sin did not come into the picture so much as the possibility of failing to be a "good person." Behavior and even fantasies that were not consistent with the kind of person he liked to think of himself as being, a decent sort of fellow, were cause for concern.

A particularly disconcerting, unwelcome yet pleasurable fantasy that presented itself one night involved a plain looking girl in his class, a smart, strong-willed character with whom he had little or no involvement. In the hypnogogic state that descended as he drifted into sleep, she was tied to the mast of a great sailing ship. He, the captain, had her at his command.

Apart from their sexual content, his fantasies had a certain aesthetic quality in which he took perverse pride. He even considered writing one down for an English composition class but thought better of it. He did, however, tell his biology teacher about the ejaculation episode during the math test.

The teacher, a middle aged woman with a pronounced limp, took it well. For his own part, he focused on the remarkable transformation of anxiety into a sexual response.

"It was like my wires got crossed," he explained.

"You think like a scientist," she replied calmly.

One morning in springtime as he walked to school, he became increasingly aware of a girl with bright blond braids who was strolling along about a block and a half ahead. He recognized her, a seventh grader, a little kid. He was in ninth. He had paid no attention to her. He didn't even know her name.

But now his eye was fixed on those blond braids. "I must catch up with her," he thought. He quickened his pace. But as he approached to maybe ten yards away, he thought better of it and lagged behind again.

"She is too young," he said to himself. "A baby."

But the blond braids had etched themselves in his mind. That night and the following day while walking to school, he thought of little else.

These, he assured himself, were not sexual thoughts but rather an appreciation of objective beauty.

How I Got To Be a Psychologist

Doll Play

I was told that I played with dolls when I was little and that more than once I wheeled some other kid's toy baby carriage in Washington Square Park. There was a picture in our family album of me doing exactly that at the age of maybe three or four. Worse, I don't recall ever finding toy soldiers interesting nor did I follow sports. Was I gay? Was I immature? Did I have a thing for babies? For carriages? Did I want to be somebody's mother?

Such possibilities would not have occurred to me and I have no memory of any of it, a matter no doubt of repression.

And that was how I got to be a psychologist.

Chickens

Before psychology there were chickens. We owned a summer house, a lovely shack in Brentwood, Long Island, a rural, multi-ethnic town at the time. The primary population was Irish Catholic that was centered around St. Joseph's Academy, a formidable institution which, because it was exotic to a New York Jewish Atheist, naturally aroused my curiosity but I never saw the inside of it.

The newer residents were Russian emigres, White Russians, I imagine. They hung out at Mr. Apatov's guest house, a somber establishment on First Avenue and Third Street where people waved their hands and argued expansively in their impenetrable tongue as they huddled around the wooden, pitched-roof radio with short-wave bands to hear the news from Europe.

Our clapboard house was bought by my parents at a bargain price in the early Depression years. It was situated on a one acre plot on the corner of Fourth Avenue and Second Street. We kept chickens during the summer just for the fun of it at first; later because of the war effort. The war did not begin until, depending on how you count, 1937, 1939 or 1941.

We first bought chickens maybe in 1935, or 1936. Our chicken involvement became serious during most of the war years, until 1944. That was when I was thirteen.

We raised chickens because my father had always wanted to be a farmer and had studied agriculture but ended up a shopkeeper in Greenwich Village and was able to take up farming only in the summertime in Brentwood.

So, each summer we had many chickens on that tiny farm. I was responsible for their care more than anyone else in the family. I loved them. They were my siblings. I was horrified at the thought of eating chickens which, I suppose, made me difficult to live with.

I made sure that the chickens were snug each evening in the chicken house, the one that Cousin Boris built. They had to be locked up because foxes were always on the prowl. Chicken lives were thus constantly at risk. Fortunately, our chickens hopped onto their roost willingly, even happily, at night for the most part but I do remember occasionally having to chase them in.

Was that really necessary? I wonder. Maybe it was because of the long summer days. They did not get to bed until nine-thirty or so which was very late for chickens as well as for a boy my age.

One evening I came down a fever followed by several unfortunate circumstances that occurred at once. It was about eight o'clock and a rain storm had begun with massive torrents of rain that descended in slobby drops.

"I *gotta* get those chickens to bed!" I screamed as I headed for the door.

"You are *sick* and are *not* going out in this weather," my mother not unreasonably shouted back.

"*I'll* catch them!" Grandma Jenny screamed. Off she went, overweight, red-faced, huffing, puffing; skirt, blouse and kerchief flying in the wild, wet wind; chickens squawking, scattering across the yard just like a flock of little grandmothers, my Grandma Jenny gasping for breath.

"Your heart! Momma! Your heart!" my mother hollared.

Dizzy with fever, reason buried deep in a sorry temper tantrum, screaming and kicking, I escaped my mother's firm grasp and scampered outdoors in my bare feet, the rain descending in wild and windy torrents.

Fortunately, it was but a warm rain; a mere summer deluge.

In no time, five minutes or maybe six, I managed to scare each and every one of those at-risk chickens to the dry safety of their coop and returned to the house, proud, defiant and beaming.

"Change into dry pajamas," my mother said wearily, "and get right to bed."

Grandma sat on a kitchen chair, wheezing and wiping her brow.

And that was how I got to be a psychologist ...chickens ....

Bozo

I was five. Right out of the blue, Grandma Jenny took it upon herself to buy me a puppy. Ignoring customers and greatly annoying my parents, she presented him to me at their exotic store, the Russian Yarmarka on 50 West 8th Street.

I fell in love at once. Bozo was then quite young, probably no more than a month and a half. He was mostly brown with some black spots. He wiggled joyously and kissed me on the face.

My parents were more than skeptical. "Oh, Ma!" my mother said in her most exasperated voice, "Who told you to buy him a *dog*? Who has time for dogs? Who is going to feed it? Who is going to walk it?

"I will," I said.

★★★★

My father remained in the City each week to run the store. He would drive up to join us in the country on the weekends.

Grandma, my mom, Bozo and I took the train together—and a magnificent, harumphing steam train it was—to Brentwood. Bozo slept in a cardboard box that rested on my lap.

Bozo was a great friend. He and I chased each other around the yard. We stomped all over the garden, too, but since it was early springtime, my father had not yet planted his customary potatoes, tomatoes, dill, peppers or cucumbers so it didn't matter.

One day I had a bunch of dog biscuits in my pocket and held them out one at a time. "Jump!" I shouted. Bozo jumped for each that I offered. He did this over and over again with admirable grace and pleasure.

"I taught him a trick!" I shouted to Grandma.

But Bozo was getting tired and so was I. It is clear in retrospect that we kept at it too long. He took a final leap up as high as he could to reach the biscuit in my hand but missed and his sharp puppy teeth tore into the crook of my arm just inside my elbow. Blood poured, not a whole lot but enough to scare me.

My mother saw at once what had happened. She grabbed me, stuffed me into the car and rushed me to Dr. Mollinoff who gave me three stitches. I cried as much for Bozo as for the wound and the stitches.

The scars are still visible over seventy-five years later.

When my father joined us that evening, he and my mother decided, despite my pleas to the contrary, to dispense with Bozo at the animal shelter in the next town.

"It was not his *fault!*" I wailed. No one paid the slightest attention.

Disaster! Catastrophe! Injustice! An insult to me, Bozo and Grandma!

A betrayal of the relationship that Bozo and I had achieved!

… And that is how I got to be a psychologist….

Advice

The daughter of immigrants, Sophie, my mother, was swept up in the art, social service and progressive education scene of the Lower East Side during the first quarter of the 20th century. Included was the Henry Street Settlement and its offspring, the Neighborhood Playhouse, and its affiliated children's camp in Schoharie, New York, where she spent summers as an arts and crafts counselor.

Although she and my father ran a store, the Russian Yarmarka, during their married lives, she always considered herself to be an artist and a teacher, a woman of good sense and excellent taste.

She was trained in preschool education by the Ethical Culture Society and taught kindergarten for a couple of years in their school on Central Park West.

It was because of her that I was sent to progressive schools—Bank Street Kindergarten, City and Country School, Little Red Schoolhouse and, finally, the Elisabeth Irwin High School—all influenced strongly by the work of John Dewey.

The course of my professional life was thus determined ... or so it would seem.

"Hey, mom and dad," I announced after graduating college and subsequently flailing about a bit in advertising, journalism and business eventually to discover considerable satisfaction in camp counseling. "Guess what? I've decided to be a *teacher!*"

"A teacher?" my mother said in her full dysphoric voice. "Why a teacher? Teachers are overworked, underpaid and spend their lives under the thumb of impossible bureaucrats."

"Hmm," I thought ... and then, in full ignorance of what it is exactly that psychologists do, I headed to Teachers College, Columbia, for a degree or two in clinical psychology... thus opening the door to happiness, independence and an okay income as needed.

III

Boston

The Harbor

Mary and I stopped at a restaurant that was perched high on a wharf in Boston Harbor. Seagulls whirled and vaulted, plunged and cawed. Wind blew gently over tiny waves and ripplets. Springtime sun pierced the dirt-gray water.

"We have never lived on a houseboat," Mary mused. "I wonder why not."

"But we knew people who did," I reminded her.

"It would have been fun to live on a houseboat," she said. "But if we had, I would never have been able to keep a garden."

"We haven't lived on an island either," I continued. "We have always loved islands.'

"It is lonely on an island," she said, "and impractical. Going to town for groceries and to see friends would be a big deal."

"What if the island were here in Boston Harbor?" I countered, "and only a ten minute ferry ride to the T?"

"That might work," she admitted. "But who would want to live on an island or even a mountaintop in bad weather?"

"No, no, no, no!" I retorted. "Not bad weather. Never. The point is that we are talking about a retreat, not a home, not a life, only a point of observation from which the world might properly be assessed. If we remain too long, it becomes a real world of its own and we lose perspective. It is only from a distance, from an island or a mountaintop, that we can see ourselves with anything like clarity."

"You are talking like a shrink again," she said. "I thought you had retired."

"Do you remember," I continued, ignoring her, "when that guidance counselor—what was his name?—and I wanted to set up a school for errant children on an island in Boston Harbor, an errant child's shrink-school for meditation and penance, a 'penitentiary,' we thought we would call it."

"What would have been your program?" she asked.

"We didn't have any," I said. "We didn't even think of a *particular* island. All we had in mind was the *idea* of an island."

"Why an island?"

"Why *not* an island?" I said. "An island is a piece of land removed from the hustle and bustle, the *sturm* and the *drang*, of the workaday world. It is a cloister that provides peace conducive to making sense of everything in the real world that is otherwise nonsensical. A mountaintop would, of course, do just as well."

"Can't a person simply shut one's ears to nonsense, take a few deep breaths and consider life as it is lived?"

"Sure. We can lock ourselves in the bathroom, sit on the pot, and let the meditations flow. That should work. Or, we might meditate out loud in a shrink's office hoping for enlightenment. Those are both islands or mountaintops in their own ways. It's just that real islands and mountaintops tend to be more pleasing esthetically and more fun to inhabit than toilets or shrinks' offices. They are gardens, wombs, holy places. They bring us back to the places of our birth.

"Would you be alone in your paradise?"

"Some of the time. Sure. But too much aloneness leads to lunacy which is exactly what we want to avoid or, once infected, to cure. A requirement is to have a few other people readily available with whom to enjoy life and to join with us in the exploration of everything whether personal or natural."

"A Shakespearian forest!" she exclaimed.

"Exactly. But only for brief and infrequent stays."

"So, in your view a good shrink is to provide a time–limited, occasional space for contemplation with little regard for wise words and interpretations."

"Yes," I continued not missing a beat, "a good shrink is rather like a landlord, the person who provides the space. Or better, a theater director who designs the *mis-en-scene*, or an architect or city planner who creates the frame in which the action is to take place; or, still better, an anthropologist who takes us to where we have never thought to be and where few if any of our habits bring forth customary responses from the locals. And what about a camp counselor who wisely creates a salutary ambience in the cabin?"

"Or God," she concluded sarcastically.

"No gods required," I countered. "In my fantasy it is the client who leads, who invents the language, who writes the script, who says the words and sings the ultimate song."

The waitress arrived with our check. We paid and wandered off.

Playroom 81

Once upon a time at the Harvard Graduate School of Education, a committee was formed that became known as "The Shadow Faculty." It was composed of professors, graduate students and a variety of others including myself. Born of "The Harvard Social Studies Project," its leader was Dr. Donald Oliver, contentious-curriculum-creator-crank-and-argumentative-iconoclast; a great man. The name, "Shadow Faculty," was derived from a British governmental device, an institution known as the "Shadow Cabinet." The idea was that the party out of power prepares a list of people to fill each cabinet position so that when the government currently in power inevitably loses a confidence vote, the new crew steps in and takes the reins of government with not a moment's loss.

The 1960s, Boston: The consensus was that the Boston schools were moribund. Aggressive right wing attorney Louise Day Hicks, staunchly opposed to desegregation, was chair of the Boston School Committee. Teaching methods were famously antiquated. Discipline was administered by swatting the offending student on the hands with a bamboo stick, a "rattan," often drawing blood. Protests flourished. Racial conflict peaked. Parents took to the streets. Busing of black children to more humane suburban schools began.

By 1973, Judge W. Arthur Garitty would rule that Boston had violated the law by the *de facto* segregation of its students.

Members of the Shadow Faculty—I for one—believed that the Revolution was at hand and that the Boston Schools were moribund.

It was therefore incumbent upon us to design a new and better, post revolutionary school system.

I had been a school psychologist employed by the Newton Public Schools for five years before becoming a research associate at the Harvard Graduate School of Education. In the latter capacity my task was to design a mental health program for the Boston Schools encompassing guidance and counseling and, among other things, addressing such problems as low motivation, absenteeism, emotional distress, lack of direction, low self-esteem, delinquency and violence.

The task of the Shadow Faculty was to conduct an "action research," study and resulting design not limited to the library and laboratory but centered rather smack in the thick of the community, in schools, homes, churches and businesses.

That suited me fine.

The *ad hoc* counseling theory that guided me and my colleague, Jay Clark, graduate student at the School of Ed, was that making the deviant student into a *recipient* of services, was counterproductive. A better goal, we thought, would instead be the inclusion of all parties, student, faculty and administration, into responsible community membership. Assuming the best, we predicted, would result in the best. We were further convinced that a positive outcome must be manifest from the very first moment of intervention.

Practically, that meant that the marginal child would from the start be given responsibility for the betterment of others, responsibility that we predicted would bring the gratitude of the community—rather than anger or banishment—to the offender.

So one bright clear morning in early fall, Jay and I hopped on our bicycles and rode through the Mission Hill Housing in Boston. Jay I were colleagues. We designed the program that we hoped would someday be instituted.

"Hey, look!" a little boy yelled. "Men on bicycles!" (That was long ago, a time when only children rode bicycles.) "Hi, kids," we shouted back. "How- ya doing?"

"Where can we find Mrs. Searcy?" we asked.

Before we arrived, we had interviewed the manager of Mission Hill plus a local priest. Both told us that in their opinion Mrs. Searcy was the key community leader.

We knocked on Mrs. Searcy's door. She was a gracious woman surrounded by a pile of children of varying ages. She welcomed us. We explained our purposes. She was receptive but explored our plans with good questions. "You plan to have juvenile delinquents run a day care center for our *children*?" she asked in a steady, skeptical voice. "I don't think that's a very good idea."

We forged ahead with our plans anyway. The project manager donated a building basement to us; we convinced community volunteers to clean it out and fix it up; then we asked local clergy, community center directors and teachers to refer questionable teenagers.

We interviewed the teenagers and described the jobs that we had in mind for them. It was only a matter, we explained, of keeping little kids busy for an hour or so after school.

The teenagers liked the idea.

Then we spoke with the mothers that Mrs. Searcy had suggested to us.

The Searcys lived on the north side of Parker Street. They and their friends were black. White families lived on the south side of the same street. There was little overlap between people on one side and the other. But we talked with mothers—and occasional fathers—on both sides, usually together.

People generally were quite receptive. Everyone seemed to think that an after school day care center was a good idea.

But about a week later, they met the scruffy teenage staff that we had lined up. There was immediate resistance. People were generally polite but the message was clear, "You Harvard guys have no idea what you are doing. There is no way that I am going to let those teenagers get at my kid."

The mothers simply took over. Jay and I were effectively removed from our leadership positions. Mrs. Searcy was now in charge. Fortunately, she was an open-minded woman who thought that potentially we had a contribution to make. From then on the mothers ran the program with help from the fathers. Jay and I were kept on as consultants to the parents—and counselors to the teenagers.

The mothers named the program "Playroom 81" because the basement in which it was located was at 81 Parker Street.

It ran for the three years that we were there and for some time afterward. Eventually, Jay and I left for other things. By then, the teenagers had endeared themselves to the mothers and continued to work with the children while under parental direction.

And black and white families got along well together.

Things continued that way for some years. I am not sure how many exactly.

This was a transformative period for me and, I daresay, for everyone whose lives were touched by Playroom 81.

Years later I met the now young adult granddaughter of one of the mothers. I knew her as a baby.

"How are things in Mission Hill these days?" I asked.

"It's a rough place to grow up in," she said. "Kids don't have anything like Playroom 81 any more."

Jamaica Plain ....

After the Harvard Graduate School of Education I found myself a promising job with the Massachusetts Mental Health Center. I was to be a community mental health psychologist assigned to Boston's Jamaica Plain neighborhood. A key part of my work was to acquaint myself with what I later called, "Nodes of Health," places, like Playroom 81, where young people were receiving affirmation and support despite inevitable lapses, not from professionals but from ordinary neighborhood residents.

Nick Moccia, now long deceased, was a colorful example, a mild mannered yet intense middle aged fellow reminiscent of Mel Brooks in the sincerity and charm of his speaking style. But he was not particularly funny. Nick had a unique and powerful hold on many of the teenagers in Jamaica Plain especially those who lived in the area near the locally famous "Green Elm," a candy store on the corner of Green and Elm streets run by Aram Arsenian,[2] an old guy with a foreign accent who had survived the 1913 Armenian Holocaust. Aram was known in the neighborhood as someone who gladly helps out a street kid with a coke, candy or a little food as needed. "I learned in Armenia," he said, "that we must help each other in this life."

Nick earned his income as a gigolo, "a male prostitute," one of the kids explained. Women of means would call to rent him for an evening or a few days. A male prostitute, sure, but a classy one. A gigolo emitting a sense of mild danger, maybe a crook; not actually handsome but hardly a bad fellow to be seen with in the evening; an excellent conversationalist with a bit of sex thrown in? Why not?

I had occasion to call Nick one night. A young girl from the community answered the phone and took a message. "I am Nick's secretary," she explained. "I arrange his dates for him." Years later she got a job with the phone company as a long distance operator. I know because some guy in Boston was trying to reach me person-to-person.

---

[2] Not his real name

When I answered the phone, the operator said, "Doc! Doc! Is that really you?"

There were others. Mary Wilson[3], a large, tough, volatile, highly energetic woman of Irish heritage had participated in Playroom 81. She was respected by everyone, black and white. Mary had a passion for kids. They were welcome in her living room at any time but they had to abide by her rules. She forbade drugs and came down hard on kids who stole. "I never said that I wanted a TV because if I did, kids would go into somebody's apartment and take one for me."

She continued, "I love kids," she said. "I love talking with them. But I don't let them take advantage."

There were also negative influences. Dick Lonergan[4] comes to mind. He also had a following of teenagers. But the word on the street was that Dick supplied kids with drugs and encouraged delinquent behavior. Nick thought that he probably used them to make money for himself. To my mind he was a real crook, the adult leader of criminal teenage gang with few if any saving graces.

Dick spent some months in jail during the time that I worked in the neighborhood. I visited him there once and brought him something to eat.

The Problem of Good and Evil

Jack Cahill died long ago, probably back in the early seventies. It is okay now for me to reflect on him in print. He was a cheerful Boston Irishman, potbellied, middle aged, affable and loyal to his friends. Engaging. Easy to talk with. Pleasant to be with.

Jack was a businessman and, frankly, a professional criminal as well. He was the undisputed chief of a motorcycle gang called the Red Emeralds, a local subdivision of California's Hell's Angels, a

[3] Not her real name

[4] Not his real name

seedy bunch of fellows who prided themselves on their demonstrable ferocity. They made their living by brining street drugs into Boston— I'm not sure from where; Mexico I think—and wholesaling them to retail street crooks.

Jack had only two fingers on his right hand. "Shot off in a fight," he explained.

I was a fresh-faced community mental health worker employed by the Massachusetts Mental Health Center, a Harvard teaching hospital. I was assigned to Jamaica Plain and worked in and around the neighborhood where the Red Emeralds had their headquarters. My goal was to foster community mental health, particularly among children and youth.

Jack, a fatherly sort, was, despite his profession, opposed to permitting young people access to narcotics. "If I find anybody buying stuff from us who's reselling it to kids," he told me more than once, "I send out my boys to beat the hell out of them."

Jack saw himself as someone who brings good to the world. He told me that despite rumors to the contrary, his gang was not racist. "We helped protect Martin Luther King when he came to town," he said.

One day I dropped into the gang headquarters. I needed to discuss something with Jack. Several of the boys were hanging around but I did not see him. He was neither in the kitchen nor the living room but I soon spotted him under the covers of his king-sized bed, embracing two attractive young woman at the same time. He introduced me.

"I am protecting them," he explained. "They are underage. I don't want the boys to get their hands on them."

I wondered why Jack was willing to tolerate me. I did after all represent convention and ultimately the law. The gang members tried to tell me stories of their exploits. These included intimidation, drunken brawls, even murder and rape. Were they testing me? I didn't want to hear any of it.

I asked Jack what he wanted from me. "Respectability," he said. "We are a sports club and I want us to be seen that way. My brother is an advisor to the mayor's office. I thought that I might get a job like that. I might help the city do something for the youth.

"Now you tell me, Bob," he continued, "why do you need me? What can I do for you?"

"Well," I said, "I am a mental health worker. Like you, I am interested in the youth of this city. It is obvious that your boys have an enormous influence. I thought that I might help them become as constructive in this as possible."

"Terrific!" Jack said. "We have the same goals. How can we get this thing going?"

"Here's an idea," I said. "I've taught at the Harvard Extension Program. What if I ask them to let me teach a course in child psychology to your boys?"

"I love it," Jack said.

A month later it was all set. We met in a conference room at the Massachusetts Mental Health Center. About a dozen of the boys roared up to the front door and sauntered down the corridors in their full regalia that included chains, leather jackets, beards, earrings, long hair, and tattoos. Psychoanalytically trained psychiatrists, psychologists, social workers, administrators and secretaries looked upon them with fear and loathing. I could see that the boys enjoyed every minute of it.

We sat down at the conference table and began.

"Why are you here?" I asked.

"Jack made us come," came the reply.

"Why are *you* doing this?" one of the boys asked.

"I want to help you and the Red Emeralds club become a positive influence on the youth of Boston."

One guy, I think it was Cougar, said, "But don't you know that when you deal with us, you are dealing with organized crime?"

I admitted that he had a point but I explained that I trusted them as individual human beings apart from their gang affiliation to have within themselves a desire to be seen as good people not just by the community but in their own minds.

The Massachusetts Mental Health Center was not entirely supportive of my activities. The head of our department spoke with me. "Can't you find a more appropriate place to hold your classes?" he asked.

Subsequent meetings were held in a nearby church.

Some months later I was called in to speak with my department head again. This time he was angry. "Do you really think that showing up with a delinquent kid at two in the morning in a police court," he demanded red-faced, "is appropriate behavior for a representative of the Massachusetts Mental Health Center?"

"I do," I said.

I lasted for only one year on that job. I can't say that I had a significant impact either on the Red Emeralds or on the youth of Boston but many good stories came out of the experience.

Here's one: When my book, *Fragments of a Lesson Plan*,[5] came out, The gang threw me a publishing party.

And another: I became the "official" gang shrink. Soon after Mary and I moved to Vermont with our two kids, we heard the roar of a large group of motorcycles speeding up our remote dirt road. It was the boys. They had found me. It seems that they were in the midst of a squabble and drove some five hundred miles 'round trip for me to help them settle it. I did my best.

Satisfied, they emptied our refrigerator, marched out the door, mounted their bikes and roared away into the night.

Reform

It's not that I enjoy being a bad guy—although I sometimes do. It is rather that I find pleasure in seeing the little guy win while the big guy fumes. My focus when in that mode is almost entirely on bureaucrats and officials. When they don't notice my provocation, I become impatient and try again. I confess that I nurture it.

---

[5] Beacon Press, 1971

Infantile, I know, but so is eating, sleeping or taking a warm bath. That's the way life is.

I am proud to say that I have caused trouble. My list of adversaries have included my department chairman at Boston College, the Director of The Lancaster Industrial Reform School for Girls in Massachusetts, the President of Goddard College, Vermont's Department of Children and Youth, and, more recently, "CASA," a program that recruits people to advise the courts in New Hampshire.

In most—actually in all—of these encounters I have emerged victorious, small-scale successes perhaps but successes nonetheless. I have also walked out of jobs that were not right for me and was always fortunate to find new employment waiting somewhere.

Only once was I actually fired but that was from a volunteer job. The sad fact is, however, that for the most part the actual gains from my rebellion were very small indeed.

Much of that topic is well beyond the scope of this book. Besides, if I boast about my escapes, I may seem boastful.

Nonetheless, despite such considerations I will now take a moment to reflect on one episode that, while it made my chest swell at the time, gave me pause as the years have passed. In retrospect I have come to wonder if I might have done better with less drama, media hoopla and celebrations of victory.

The story

Back in the late '60s while an Associate Professor in Psychology and Counseling (joint appointment) at Boston College, I found myself a part-time consultantship at the venerable Lancaster Industrial Reform School for Girls, America's first reform school celebrated as an alternative to slamming kids in jail. Lancaster had about four hundred inmates as I recall, a sad looking bunch of poor children ranging in age from ten or so through adolescence.

The campus, about seventy acres, was well tended. It had green grass and lots of beautiful flowers and trees. A main. house and several smaller ones were in tasteful, nineteenth century architecture; no grand dormitories. Girls had actual rooms, a few kids in each. Each noon, staff were waited on by uniformed inmates then ate civilized lunches compete with *au d'oeuvres* and tea. The headmistress/superintendent was an intelligent, well educated woman with reputedly reformist views and an impressive history. There was a rather Edwardian feel to the entire scene.

At first glance this reform school might be mistaken for a college.

Education at Lancaster prepared the girls on release for useful occupations especially those common in the 19th century. I visited a dressmaking class, for example, and another on cooking. There were also regular classrooms and a library.

The school contained some four hundred residents at the time. Ages? About ten through adolescence. I don't remember how large the staff was but I do know that I was to be the entire mental heath department. And my schedule permitted me to be there for no more than a half day a week, about three hours each Friday morning—except on holidays.

It was immediately apparent that most if not all of the four hundred girls had personal issues and might benefit from or, indeed, sorely required psychological help.

Despite the absurd chasm between the counseling need and the available resources, I was pleased to work there in large part because of my growing belief in the benefits that can best be found for young people in a retreat setting, an alternative to home, a place where one might obtain perspective on the original scene, on real life. I entertained the dream of steering this institution further in this useful direction.

I sang "Tiptoe Through the Tulips" while driving to work.

I advised the headmistress that, given the number of potential clients, we should move in three directions at once. First, I thought we should offer regular small group counseling sessions to which attendance might be required. Children might might join voluntarily. Confidentiality would, of course, be insured. I figured that I might be able to run three such groups per morning each week, each containing no more than eight counselees.

Second, I thought that I might recruit another staff member to assist in each group for the purpose of her training. This effectively would enlarge the psychology/counseling staff and enhance its potential usefulness.

Third, I would need time to supervise the staff trainees.

The headmistress agreed on all points.

We gave it a try. It started out well but disaster was just ahead.

We began with one group. The first couple of weeks went well enough. Members were assigned by the administration. I tried to get the names more or less straight and to absorb some basic information about each. A staff woman sat in with us. She said little and her face revealed less. I felt uncomfortable in her presence. The kids probably did, too, but there was little to be done about it.

Conversation was awkward at first. This was after all an unfamiliar situation for everyone, myself included. I tried loosening things up with a few jokes. And then I opened the session with the assurance that people should feel free to say what was on their minds. "What you say in this group," I assured them, "stays in this group. There will be no spreading gossip afterwards. You cannot get into trouble for anything that you say in here. It is our private place."

Faces were blank. I did not know what if anything came across.

Things went along well enough for some weeks. Gradually the girls became more trusting; more conversational. Stories were told about life at the school, some were unremarkable but some had to do with scapegoating, fights; brutality—including the gang rape of one of the girls with a broom handle.

Then we hit a wall.

An angry eleven year year old was absent from the group one day. Where was she? I asked the headmistress. "Oh? She is in solitary confinement," came the answer.

Solitary confinement for a disturbed eleven year old?

I went to see the kid. I was cautioned by the staff member in charge of her unit that a visit, while permissible given my position, required that I keep the door ajar—presumably to protect her from me.

The room was bare of furniture, toys and books. The child, dressed in a smock, sat on the floor, listless as if in a stupor. She had two knitting needles in her hand.

"I am going to kill myself," she said.

I took the knitting needles away and questioned her about the trouble she was in but the conversation went nowhere. I did learn, however, that she had been in solitary for a full week.

I returned to the headmistress. "Why is an eleven year old in solitary confinement?" I demanded, my voice shaking.

She was there, I was told, because of something that she had said in my counseling group the week before. (This was years ago and I cannot now remember what it was.) In any event, the attending staff member had reported it to the headmistress despite having agreed to the rule that "what is said in this group stays in this group." And, "we cannot get in trouble for anything that is said here."

I uttered a word or two of alarm but managed to contain myself.

As it happened, the school had an important visitor that day. I was introduced to her at lunch.

"I am an investigator from the Massachusetts State Senate," she explained. "We are concerned about conditions in our reform schools. I have come today as part of an ongoing investigation."

"I am very pleased to see you," I said. "There is a kid that I would like you to meet."

I took her to the eleven year old. They spoke for a while. The investigator thanked me as we walked back to the main house.

It was clear then that my time at the Lancaster Industrial Reform School was over. Done with. I was convinced that once my role in the investigation became known, I would be discharged.

"Well," I figured, "since the end has come, I might just as well make the most of the situation."

When I returned home, I called the Boston Globe and a television station. Soon our house was filled with reporters and a television crew.

There were many people working to improve juvenile corrections in Massachusetts at the time. I was only one of them. It was in the spirit of the times. Mental hospitals were also being examined critically then.

Some eight years after the episode I have related, all of the reform schools and mental hospitals in the state were closed.

It was surely a victory. Hands down.

The problem was that, while we—the citizens—were assured that the cost savings would be invested in community programs both in corrections and mental health, the promise was never realized. Instead the institutional savings landed in the general fund.

Our victory indeed turned out to be a hollow one. And the children and patients of Massachusetts were left in significant ways worse off than they were before.

For one thing, the beautiful campus of the Lancaster Industrial Reform School for Girls slipped into disuse and never got close to becoming the retreat center I had imagined.

That's the way the ball bounces, I suppose.

Would I have done better to contain myself and work within the system, biding my time, eventually to help redesign the institution and influence it to be a more helpful resource?

Maybe. But institutions of this sort are very resistant to change. It is never clear whether the person will reform the system or the system will change the person into a sad shadow of his or her former self now at one with the harmful entity.

A Generous Gift from Boston College

The upside of the story was that Boston College took my celebrity in Lancaster and another matter—The Globe reported that I had testified against corporal punishment in Boston's public schools—as indications that I must be got rid of.

Rumor had it that the College president received a phone call from an alum: "As long as you keep a S.O.B. like Belenky on your faculty, you won't get another penny from me."

That was fine. By then I was more than ready to leave. Although I enjoyed the teaching during the previous four years, I hadn't found many real colleagues at B.C. and I missed the frothy radicalism of the Harvard Graduate School of Education.

I was now considering penurious Goddard College as my next professional landing.

So ... as I was bidding farewell to students and faculty, minding my business, packing my bags, heading for the door and preparing to hit the road ... a professor from the law school dropped in to point out that the method chosen to can me was utterly illegal. He wanted to put a stop to it—*pro bono*—for the sake of the entire faculty.

So ... He and I met with the institution's president during which we were assured that the procedure had been B.C.'s customary practice since its founding in 1863.

"Be careful," my attorney friend warned. "If that is indeed the case, B.C. will be liable for breach of contract suits stemming from 1863." The president then gulped and with no further ado offered me a generous $15,000 if I would just shut up and get lost. I accepted immediately; gratefully.

I found myself a job at Boston University for the following year.

The year after that it was off to Goddard where, once in Vermont, Mary and I put Boston College's welcome gift to good use. We purchased the land that became The Clearing.

"Is it time for lunch, Mary?" I asked while typing the previous paragraph.

"I'll call you when it's ready," she said.

IV

Vermont

Mary, the kids, dog and I moved to Vermont in part because we imagined that it would be a good place for our family to live and to find a lovely venue for my reparative camp obsession.

A camp? Yes. I was convinced then and still am that camps are inherently therapeutic; powerfully, pleasantly, automatically redeeming. No need for a therapist or a medicine man. Required only are blue skies, clean air, compatible company, a simple shelter and a sensible host. A camp, I said, is a variation on the theme of pub; the counselor, its landlord, all told a merry place but absent the libations.

And that is just what we did. We created an camp in the woods intended to promote happiness and civility. And it worked ... pretty much that way.

That has been my contribution.

The Fifth Essence

Essence #1: Biology
Essence #2: Play/Support
Essence #3: Work/Contribution to Others
Essence: #4: History
Essence: #5: Reflection

Reflection, the Fifth Essence, is what this book is about.

The purpose of Reflection is to make sense of the workaday world which subsequently may be reentered armed with an enhanced supply of coping skills.

Reflection may take place in dreams, art, theater, ritual, music, dance, poetry, literature, religion, and insanity—indeed in virtually any relatively benign temporary absence from the workaday world into a time and place of contemplation; a retreat, a vacation; even a psychotherapist's office.

Reflection has been the Clearing's signature offering.

Asinine Rx

After Mary and I married, we naturally thought about having children. In an attempt to facilitate the process, Julie, Mary's mother, promised, "I will give one donkey to each child that you produce."

I cannot remember exactly why she said that. I cannot ask her. She is long dead. She probably just liked donkeys. Or children. But motivation should not matter. A promise is a promise.

We soon produced two children, Alice and Michael, good kids once, now middle aged with adult children of their own.

Although Julie was a trustworthy person, the donkeys never arrived. I do not hold this against her. She must have had her reasons.

In any event, time passed. Some years later I became the *maître d'* of the Clearing, the retreat center for children and teen-agers that I have been writing about. It was a camp, much like any other camp except that nobody stayed for more than a day or so—but they could and did return occasionally or periodically—and the emphasis was on getting one's life straightened out. I was also the counselor; counselor in two senses, camp counselor and the person one goes to for consultation on handling life's problems.

Almost every day we hosted one to a half dozen young people. We talked a lot or took psychological tests some of which we invented. But we also had a good time doing what the season called for: swimming, boating, skiing, fishing, writing, drawing and so on. It was a nice scene and the kids enjoyed it. I did, too.

The Clearing was a full mile into the woods without much of a road—until recently—and not far from a remote, underused and utterly gorgeous lake. At first we had no road at all. We arrived by bushwacking, boat, snowshoe or ski, carrying our food and equipment with us.

One day I had an epiphany, "Wouldn't it be great if we had a horse? At least one of us could then ride, bringing the food and equipment with him or her?"

I called Peter Hood, our insurance agent, and ran the idea by him.

"No way," Peter said. "You would not be able to afford the premiums. It is an entirely impractical idea."

I thought about this for a while and then it occurred to me: The donkeys! Grandma Julie's donkeys!

I called Peter again. "Donkeys?" I asked. "What about donkeys?"

"Let me research this," Peter said. "I'll get back to you."

The next day Peter called. "Donkeys are the way to go," he said. "The insurance industry has no actuarial data on the accident risk associated with donkeys. There will therefore be no premium increase."

"Thank you, Peter!" I said.

During the following weeks I poured over newspaper ads for donkeys. There were none. I inquired of everyone who might possibly have a lead, altogether an onerous task. But I persisted because I was highly motivated. In no more than a couple of months, I was told by a farmer friend that a donkey was for sale in the next town.

I followed the directions given me and arrived at a beautiful place well hidden from public view. The donkey was a gorgeous white female named Angelina owned by a recently deceased sister of Mme Chiang Kai-shek. Angelina was now being cared for by the fellow in charge of the estate. She had a brother, Sam, who was also for sale. Both donkeys were polite, charming and obviously civilized. I agreed at once to purchase them.

The caretaker had them brought to the Clearing the next day.

Sam and Angelina were a helpful addition to our offerings both from practical and professional perspectives. When we held a session, parents would drive their children through the woods as far as they could where they came to a rail gate beyond which was a huge fenced-in area that encompassed the meeting house and grounds. Sam and Angelina—who heard us coming because they had very acute hearing—met us at that gate whereupon the children packed their things on the donkeys' backs and walked beside them down the hill to the activity area. Occasionally a child would sit astride a donkey who raised no objection.

The donkeys were my adjunct therapists along with a good dog and a human assistant—somebody who children appreciated, in all likelihood a counselor in the sense of "camp counselor," not therapist. I myself have always resisted being a therapist. I believe that there are roles in life that are far more therapeutic. However, I must confess that I have never been clear about what a therapist is or might do beyond what the donkeys and the dog did.

We had a long, wooden dining table set out on the deck in front of the house. We often ate our lunch there. That got to be a problem. The donkeys were always out to snarf a bit of food, a sandwich or a desert. There was no fence separating the table from the lawn where the donkeys hung out. As a result, our meals were interrupted by a big, white donkey-head thrust out into the middle of the group soliciting anything edible.

We soon issued what became a famous edict: "No feeding donkeys at the table."

We kept those donkeys for some five or six years, finally selling them when I prepared for retirement. During all that time Sam and Angelina remained consistently polite and respectful. They were also warm-hearted. They particularly enjoyed giving short rides to children and were cooperative about carrying baggage. And they were fun-loving. They had a great sense of humor.

An example of donkey humor: Sometimes if you wanted to catch them, they would wait patiently until you were no more than a foot away. Then they would bolt suddenly and gallop off for a good distance, stand still and wait for you to try again all the while laughing under their asinine breath.

Wet Pants

On a raw day one late October, Rachel, our then dog, and I hiked out to the Clearing to tend to some minor repairs. There was a light cover of snow on the ground and a brilliant panoply of autumn leaves above our heads. The sky was azure; cloudless.

That was long ago. The building we had then was a soaring two-story, wooden structure with a generous deck extending from the upstairs combination dormitory and living room.

I glanced up at the deck and noticed a child's snow pants draped over the railing. A large downstairs window was open. I unlocked the front door and entered. Inside the cold was penetrating but the house was tidy. Everything seemed to be in its place. I was not aware of missing items.

We had no indoor plumbing at the time so there was no possibility of broken pipes. Yet there had obviously been a break-in.

I climbed the stairs. The dormitory, too, was in good shape; no sign of damage. I then walked out onto the deck. The snow pants were the only sign of anything amiss.

It dawned on me: These snow pants belong to Annie[6], a large, bossy ten year old.

"Ha!"

A couple of days later, I happened to be in Barre on an errand. Barre is the small Vermont city were Annie lived in a public housing

---

[6] Not her real name.

project with her mother, her stepfather and two slightly younger step sisters. I brought the snow pants along with me. I dropped in on the household to return them and to confront Annie with the crime. Annie was the obvious perpetrator.

"Thank you for bringing me my ski pants," Annie smiled.

"You are welcome," I said. "But," I added, "I am very upset that you broke into the Clearing."

"I didn't break in," she mumbled.

"Okay. How did your ski pants manage to get on the deck railing?"

"I put them there to dry. I fell in a brook."

"But," I continued, "you climbed in through a window. That's called 'breaking in.'"

"Listen, Bob: We swept the floors, we did the dishes and put everything away just the way you like it," she said.

It was hard to know what to say next. "How did you get out there?" I asked.

"Me and my sisters rode on our bicycles," she said.

"But," I blurted. "The distance! Nine miles each way. And the traffic? You are only ten and your sisters are younger."

"We were okay," she said.

"You broke in!" I repeated, returning to the issue at hand.

"We *didn't* break in. It is our house, too, you said," she mumbled on the verge of tears. "We put everything away. We washed the dishes. We swept the floor. We did everything right," she added, "just like you want us to."

Technological Advances

In the summer when we began to build the first Clearing house, the earliest materials were shipped across the lake on an old motorboat that I purchased for the that use. We hired local teenagers to carry the lumber and things bushwacking up the hill to the building site thus creating our first path. One of those teenagers later became the principal of a next town's elementary/high school.

That winter, to complete the job, fixtures needed to be brought in including two sinks, a kitchen stove and a bathtub. We hired a local neighbor, a woodsman. He worked with an addicted horse who was rewarded with a Lucky Strike for doing as he was told. The horse gratefully devoured each proffered cancer stick.

The culmination of all this came when the woodsman hitched the addicted horse to the bathtub which he loaded with such necessary items as a kerosene cook stove and two sinks, one for the bathroom and the other for the kitchen.

The horse struggled on command and managed to haul the loaded bathtub the full mile over the snow to the Clearing building site. He was amply rewarded every few minutes for his efforts.

The following winter when we were in full operation, trash would sometimes be carried out by placing the can on a sled to which we would hitch Boris, our dog at the time, a Norwegian Elkhound. Elkhounds are genetically disposed to hauling.

Communications: At first we had no way of communicating with the outside world, a dangerous situation. There were no cell phones in those days. I addressed the problem by purchasing a CB radio and wiring it to a car battery, an awkward but serviceable solution. Some years later, as the phone company was putting in a new line on the nearby road, they offered to send off a branch down to the Clearing at a bargain price. We accepted and as a result have had excellent phone service there for quite a while. Eventually we had DSL wifi added thus rendering us very much part of the world that we had escaped from. But we did not use it when we were in session.

Water: At first we had no water. We used an outhouse. For cooking, we filled buckets in the lake where the water was certifiably clean and carried them up the hill. Eventually we decided to dig a well. I contracted with the dowser association in the next town. The daughter of the founder, a certified young water-witch, searched with her forked stick for a source. She found a good one and we have never been without water since.

Electricity: For our first few years we used kerosene lamps. But I soon found that I came home after a few nights with a throbbing headache. Solar electricity was just becoming known. We thought we might give it a try.

Our first system involved a tiny solar panel and direct current. But it was more than adequate to power one or two small lightbulbs. However, I ignorantly hitched the contraption to my early-version, alternating current, laptop computer which it instantly destroyed.

But we upgraded the system over the years. By the time of the sale, we had a sophisticated system including two arrays, six panels, twelve three-foot tall batteries, alternating current and a generator back-up. And an electric grass mower the batteries of which were charged by our solar panels.

We had all the electricity we needed.

And we had a very nice road right up to the main house.

Everything was modern, functioned well and exemplary. We were pleased although we missed something of the rugged romance of the early days. But we were less rugged by then ourselves.

Perspective

I do not like the term, "Therapy." It implies that the patient, the child, the target of the treatment, is sick-in-the-head and that the procedure to be followed is curative through medication or, in the case of psychotherapy, through words that have a medicative effect.

I much prefer "treatment" which suggests a "treat," something delicious to eat, maybe ice cream.

The power of what we did at the Clearing lay in our abject denial, in our stubborn assumption of the normality, charm, indeed the virtue of the child at hand rather than in his or her pathology or moral failings; in our strident reluctance to place personal blame, and in our geographical mindset—our conviction that solace resides in physically avoiding—or at least gaining perspective on—unhappy circumstances by temporary removal to a safe and remote haven where the workaday world may be viewed as through a telescope in the absence of threat, in blissful safety, drama and adventure.

The confusion or pain experienced back home may be coped with in our Olympian setting through the vehicle of the imagination supported by benign nature, good people and a brief respite from intolerable circumstances. The Clearing becomes the place to put things in perspective, achieved by standing cooly aside to study the workaday world.

The Clearing model is situational. Treatment is removal from people who support or afflict us and all that sustains a sense of who we are. It consists of immersion in a momentary utopia that offers a glimpse of who we might be and to practice new ways of being.

Once in this unlikely place, a person is faced with the obligation to explore new habits and reach out to new relationships with everything, animate and inanimate. In this way unimagined ways of being are revealed and may gradually even be adopted.

The Clearing, our fairyland laboratory was where perspective became possible and where real life might be viewed with clarity but at a convenient distance.

Tramping through the woods to arrive at in our Eden was not unlike climbing a great mountain from whose summit great vistas unfold. People and circumstances that previously loomed in our faces are now tame; Lilliputian. Lions have become kittens; hurricanes, summer showers.

When the imagination is so messed with, the major question becomes: How is one to maintain the new prospective after returning to real life?

Sometimes conversations of this issue took place although more often the answer was unspoken yet intuited. The new self that began gradually to emerge at the Clearing materialized, unbidden, back home. The Clearing simply provided the impetus for resilient elements to take fragile root. With luck, the new ways of dealing with the world proved practical, confidence building and self-perpetuating; confidence leading to success and success to greater confidence.

Follow-up support was of course desirable. If we had the staff and the funding we could have done more. But we did some. When kid-clients were local, they returned often and I was able to visit them occasionally at home.

What I am describing is no more than the value of release from the workaday self with change of locus: a respite, a new place to live, a new school, a new job, or other ways of altering the conditions that determine the sense of who we are or might become. Assuming a role in a theatrical production, another path to the same goal, comes to mind. In each instance the self, challenged, grows stronger, more resilient: healthier. The major difference is that the Clearing was a place designed to be other than real life. It was a laboratory, a vacation, a temporary absence from *la vie quotidienne*.

Caution: If one were to remain at the Clearing for too long—a week, a season or a lifetime—there is the likelihood that old habits would reestablish themselves. But with an intentional series of alternations between the real world where one's life is mostly lived and the brief, magical laboratory, a cycle of experimentation and growth may be generated whether or not within one's awareness. There is then the possibility that our better angels will spread their wings and gradually ascend.

A Gingerbread Tale

Hansel and Gretel, starving at home and unhappy with their stepmother and the poverty of their lives, tried to escape but found themselves facing the further misfortune following on their discovery of the gingerbread house where they faced mortal danger. Still, it was an adventure and to the extent that it worked out well in the end and, thanks to the little girl's quick wits, it turned out to be a growth experience. Nobody was eaten, the children collected a fortune in jewels that enabled them and their dear father to live happily ever after.

The Clearing was a benign witch's house. Unhappy children arrived to find surcease from misery and the strength to cope with intolerable circumstances. That was the theory. And sometimes the fact.

The witch's house, like the Clearing, was the locus of an alternative family. But the witch, sadly, was not the sort of parent substitute one normally recommends. Nonetheless, her house was where Hansel and Gretel came into their own. It was a magic venue however unpleasant. The children emerged from it into maturity, strong enough not merely to master their own lives but to feed and care for their well meaning but ineffective dad.

Similarly, children appeared on the Clearing doorstep and entered into our magic world, seeking there to find surcease from one monstrous thing or another in the real world. We specialized in providing the trappings of danger but psychological and edible nourishment as well and time to master the situation whatever it was.

Thus: It was not so much *talking* about problems as *experiencing*, however briefly, mastery of their lives and in so doing perhaps discovering that mastery of life is itself a goal actually within reach.

We did many things at the Clearing that may have been helpful to the children but are not included under the psychotherapy rubric by most people. We took trips, for example. There were several times I recall when we piled everyone in the car and headed for Montreal for a pizza, returning to Vermont that evening. The kids I best remember came from a group home where they lived together. These were children of the rural poor, foster kids from marginal families some of whom had never been as far from home as Montpelier. Montreal amazed them. They especially loved the Metro and took delight in riding up and down the escalators.

We usually had one staff member beside myself on duty even with a single child or several in a tiny group. It is hard to work alone with active children and at the same time to pay close attention to all that goes on.

The Clearing had an educational component: We invited occasional guests. We brought artists and poets to visit us. And an occasional actor, musician or politician; one guy, an old, clever, unclean folkloric character whom Goddard students were supporting for State Senator. He told the kids a moving rendition of his life story. A forester visited occasionally to take the kids tramping through the woods. A disagreeable ex-con from Boston showed up once— uninvited and not as part of the program. There may even have been educational value in meeting him.

We canoed and skied and spent hours talking quietly around the campfire.

There was not much therapy in the ordinary sense going on. The active ingredient was rather the collection of experiences, some more to the point than others but together forming the framework of a new, unaccustomed life.

On the other hand, we did discuss problems and their possible resolution, sometimes individually, sometimes in small groups but almost always unscheduled. The conversations emerged from whatever else we were doing.

There were occasional formal discussions, too, many with the kids and others that included parents, school personnel or state social workers. These last were sometimes stressful because for children who were in custody, the workers were known to have considerable legal power that ran butt-headed into the sore wounds of their clients.

Sometimes we used the Clearing as a benign venue for non-custodial fathers to spend time with their children while I encouraged normal conversation between them as we fished, hiked, cut wood, prepared meals or did the dishes together.

With pride in our audacity, we occasionally pushed the limits of the conventional by permitting skinny-dips in the lake on moonlit summer nights. Sometimes at dinner I even poured each kid a glass of red wine while offering words aimed at associating wine with conviviality rather than loneliness, misery and addiction. Many of our clients came from families where alcoholism was a major issue.

There also took place what one might expect of the Clearing to the extent that it was a mental health clinic. I administered tests, WISC sand Stanford-Binets, Rorschachs and TATs, figure drawings, Bender Gestalts and MMPIs. I dutifully quoted the results in reports that I wrote to parents, schools, and the courts. To the extent possible I tried to render them intelligible to the child him or herself.

I testified in court. I made referrals and consulted with teachers, social workers and guidance counselors in both public day schools and boarding schools.

We in fact had two streams of clients: Local Vermont kids, mostly poor and socially marginal as well as children referred by private schools, affluent to lavishly rich kids who in some ways seemed as inadequately served by their families as did the children of the poor.

We seldom had more than a half dozen kids come to the Clearing at once. The usual group was segregated, composed of members of one sector of society or the other, public or boarding schoolers. But sometimes there was an overlap, a few from one social class along with a few of another. The rich, often as unhappy as the poor although better dressed and on healthier diets. But the poor, I thought, were for the most part better able to cope with the world as it is, on the street if not in the school, although they well understood that eventual upward social mobility was unlikely.

One of my favorite activities: I asked children to write their autobiographies or to dictate them to me as I typed them out on my clunky Royal Office machine.

And we talked and talked and talked about everything—including personal problems and how to deal with them.

And we played with the donkeys and the dog.

Oh, yes, it was a lovely place; an absolute Eden.

And I, too, grew from participation.

And nobody got gobbled up by any old witch and almost everyone found their way home again.

The program evolved over the fifteen plus years of the Clearing's operation. In some ways things eventually became routinized. But the spirit remained quirky, defiant, familial and rooted in ambience rather than anything specific.

Shrinks

A small pack of kids, three or four of them, twelve or so years old as I recall, strolled down the road to the Clearing. I overheard some of their conversation.

"I hate seeing my shrink," one of them said.

"Shrinks piss me off," said another. "They are too nosy."

"A third offered that whatever his problem it's all his mother's fault anyway because she brings her stupid boyfriend home. "*She* should be seeing a shrink," he said. "Not me."

"Shrinks are a waste of time," the first kid said.

"Wait, guys," I butted in. "I'm a shrink."

"No way," came the response. "You're not a shrink. You're just somebody we can talk to."

The Clearing was (I use the past tense because we are in the process of selling the property as I write) a tract of 130 acres bordering almost seven hundred wilderness acres belonging to the Vermont Land Trust. This, in turn, is adjacent to 26,000 acres of Vermont state forest land.

It was an Eden, as I have written, within two additional Edens in the midst of which, a mile from the road, we built a house. No. Not the ordinary house that you would recognize at once as a home but rather a fanciful thing.

We in fact built three houses. The first one burned down after six years and the second one twenty years after. No one was hurt; no one was at fault. And each time, thanks to bountiful insurance, we were able to rebuild, each new building more practical, more substantial although less funky than the one before. All three were stunning in its own way.

I will tell you about the first house: Anarchic Goddard College had an architecture program going during the late 1970s. They didn't call it "architecture" probably because the AIA would object. They called it "Design" but architecture it actually was. The professor, David Sellers, an radically imaginative but plausible fellow, had his students compete for employment by the client as real architects do. I played the part of client in exchange for their services.

I was to write out my needs, discuss them with the class and agreed to judge the resulting entries, weighty responsibilities.

"I need a house in the woods, I explained, where unhappy children may feel secure and may be themselves without danger, embarrassment or more than a modicum of civilized constraints."

The winning design was a fanciful two storied structure with vertical, unfinished wood siding, huge windows, a large, meandering second story balcony and no access at all other than by bushwhacking; and neither power nor heat nor telephone nor water nor toilet. It was indeed nothing more nor less than a blank, high rise, convivial tower in the midst of a natural clearing. Dark, ancient trees loomed above it. Berry vines grew around it.

Surely it was an ideal office for the likes of the unlikely shrink that I took myself to be—as indeed I was and will surely remain to the last day of my dotage.

Consultation Rock

Last October as we were preparing to sell the Clearing, Milly, our sweet Labradoodle and I hiked through the woods down by "The Marshfield Dam," as it is called by the locals even though the official name is "Molly's Falls Pond." We went as far as the shallow beach at the Point stopping for a moment on the rock where one has a

55

stunning view of the island. I used to sit on that very rock with kids who came to the Clearing to be made happy.

A moment after we arrived, a scruffy man, aged fifty or so, followed by two teenagers, a boy and a girl, trudged the trail toward us. He smiled broadly. I recognized him at once. It was George.[7] I first met him when he was twelve or thirteen, an earnest, struggling kid trying to survive in the absence of anything but the most rudimentary family support.

"And that," he said to his children, "is the rock I told you about."

---

[7] Not his real name.

V

Help!

Ka-Boom!

This is about the time I flew into an unprofessional fury, an inexplicable event but one possibly worth exploring or at least confessing to.

An orphanage in Western Russia: Well, it's not exactly an orphanage. They call it a boarding school using the French term, "*internat.*" But many of the children there are indeed orphans although others have families. The families by and large tend to have serious problems including abuse, violence, alcoholism, criminality, neglect, illness or stark poverty.

The place is more open than an orphanage, more decent. Children are not incarcerated, they head to town on their own when they wish. Some go home on weekends. Punishment is mild and uncommon. Thus morale is higher than in real Russian orphanages; nonetheless most of the children are poor, struggling, frightened and needy.

Some years ago I suggested to the head of a fine American summer camp—that frequently sponsors overseas ventures—that they might consider an expedition to Russia for older campers. It could involve a construction project of some sort in the internat.

The director loved the idea and set up the program for the following summer. She recruited a guy to run it who had successfully led a number of outdoor adventure excursions, mountain climbing, sleeping in the wild, that sort of thing. I was to come along as an educational consultant.

But, although the leader was smart about many things, he seemed to know nothing about Russia, its history, culture nor indeed its marginal children.

As for the young people who joined the group, they were for the most part unprepared for the experience. That was our job—to prepare them, I thought. But the leader did not seem oriented in that direction and seemed uncomfortable by my presence. The volunteers must have been aware that there was stress at the leadership level.

Nonetheless, the group functioned pretty well. Some of the Americans were mature, idealistic teenagers while others were unfocused. Jokes in poor taste and nervous giggles were in the air.

We all worked hard, however, and we were tired. I know I was. The volunteers surely must have been as well. The situation was unfamiliar, often stressful, beyond the experience of most and our group never really became a solid team.

Tension mounted.

One day I exploded ... finally.

A minor incident perhaps but it got to me and everyone else.

You see, I was trying to read a story in my very basic Russian to a group of maybe a dozen restless, four and five year old Russian orphans who resisted all my efforts to calm them down and coax them into listening. Their teachers took my presence as an opportunity to absent themselves for a cup of tea. Altogether this was not a set of insurmountable problems but one that was resistant to resolution.

Three teenaged US kids sat by, passive, vaguely watching. That was okay except that one of them held a child on his lap and was tickling him, the two giggling hysterically together.

I asked our teenager to stop tickling the kid and to help me pull the group together.

He ignored me. Not once. Not twice. Several times.

Finally—I exploded.

I didn't know then nor do I know now exactly why I exploded. The volunteers not unreasonably concluded that I had gone mad.

I had.

But actually I am, most people would agree, generally seen as an even-tempered fellow who doesn't often lose it.

What occurred?

I was tired. That was part of it.

And I was upset because the children were hard to manage.

Also true. But I'd seen worse over the years and had mostly managed to maintain civility on my own part and to promote it on the part of others with no dramatic explosions.

This time, however, was different.

My recollection is that there was another factor at play in addition to fatigue. It was perhaps subtle; hidden under a cloak of fun.

It was that teenager. The volunteer. He repeatedly bounced the wildly giggling orphan boy on his knee. He did this with escalating hilarity on both their parts. The little one was being stimulated. Overstimulated. The affect of the teenager appeared to me frantic, joyless; robotic. In addition, I suspected that our American fool was deliberately sabotaging my efforts to bring order to the group. Difficult to prove these things but that's what I felt or saw or think I saw; certainly it was what I believed.

Worse ... I suspected more than that, stuff that I cannot prove.

The thought flashed by that their play had sexual undertones.

Even now, years later, I more than suspect that it did.

But how to deal with it? I did not know then nor do I now.

Nothing explicitly sexual happened, you understand. But there was that something in the air, something that I am at a loss to describe. It was, however, something sentient, palpable, unhealthy, impossible to confront, and at the very least destructive of group process.

So ... I was at cross purposes with the Group Leader, convinced that there was something the matter with our process, and annoyed at the teenagers and too tired to deal constructively with any of it.

And ... I lost it. I screamed at the teenager to shape up and get with the program; reasonable enough requests, you say. But my voice was harsh and more than half crazy.

As a result, I scared the wits out of everyone, the teenagers most of all. The orphan children—no doubt. And myself? I wonder even now about myself.

The teenager complained to the Group Leader that I was prejudiced against him and way-out nuts besides. I could think of no way to refute these charges.

So ... I let it go dammit, a chicken-ass decision that I regret to this day.

★★★★

Why do I bother with such places anyway? What am I to the children who live there? They call me "Grandpa" but I intersect only rarely and briefly with their lives. And I am *not* their grandfather. I do not remember their birthdays. I do not take them to the zoo. I do not buy them Christmas gifts. After only a very few years, I forget their names. Does my brief presence have any value at all or does it only sharpen their pain?

Accompanied as I was by a busload of wealthy young tourists flowing with clueless high spirits ... what did it then signify?

Batman

Oh, I *love* thumbing my nose at authority on behalf of the child. I adore the rebel role. Much was theater in those days, an identification with Batman. But I was, am, and in fact always have been a constitutional moderate, cautious, indeed, a deferential fellow. I have done my best to civilize the younger generation while wearing the trappings of rebellion but largely for their edification and amusement.

I confess to having worked both sides of the street. To the extent that I may have been helpful it was because I appreciate children and their foibles. I see young people by and large as charming, amusing, talented, witty and graceful rather than simply infuriating. Some of them see old people in much the same way.

Mary and I are aged. We live in a nice Quakerish retirement community, a "Geezer Ghetto." Life here is okay. If you must be put out to pasture, this is not a bad one. But I miss much … my youth and my profession.

I think about volunteering but don't think I will. Writing these memoirs is enough. It is the main task. After that, who knows?

Geezer Ghettos are Purgatory. Is next stop up … or down?

The Beach

The good-hearted volunteer, an American black woman, and I hired a "tap-tap" [pickup truck whose deck is covered with a hand-made, wooden roof] to take Haitian kids on an outing. We filled it with street children, six boys. We promised them a swim.

The boys were hungry and dressed in rags. We fed them sandwiches and sodas and we all splashed in the water. We gave them swimming lessons.

On the return trip, we all huddled together on a tap-tap bench and we asked how we could help them.

"Adopt us," they said, straight and earnest.

One of the boys was smaller than the rest and the butt of the larger boys' humor. They seemed protective of him but also were probably threatened by his obvious vulnerability and so teased him for no reason other than that he was small and afraid and that children everywhere are predisposed both to good and to evil.

The little boy said nothing and did not strike back or cry. He merely sat very close to the woman.

As our vehicle rolled into their neighborhood, the little boy jumped off the tap-tap and we saw him last wandering through the darkening, chaotic streets, dazed and alone.

Guerilla ....

I am, to be perfectly frank, not much into nature. Neither do I appreciate physical challenges. Survival? No thank you. Hiking? Tedious. Bicycling? Sticky-hot and stressful. Cross-country skiing? Exhausting. I do not know about plants, animals or fungi. I am Ferdinand the Bull, passive, feckless yet appreciative of the passing scene. I dream. I lack the will but don't care.

The wilderness for me is a fiction, a backdrop, a stage, an occasion, a fantasy, a potential, a rendering rather than an original; a blank slate, a virgin ball field on which no game has yet been played; a dream; utter darkness yet to manifest enlightenment, a silence, a mystery; scary yet oddly welcoming, a world within or upon which nothing stirs but yet where the future throbs in expectation, where significant action is imminent. Nothing is provided but possibility.

Mine was a guerrilla operation, intentionally so. I picked fights with social service authorities. I testified against their ill-conceived demands for child custody. I consider it obscene to remove a child from the home of his or her parents, no matter how marginal, to place him or her with a stranger in an alien universe and one often as abusive as the original.

Why can't we work with the parents? Help them make a life? Assume responsibility for themselves and their progeny?

And so we created our homeland in the woods, an imaginary family in an imagined dimension of time and space that enhanced but did not compete with the family of origin. We lived our dream and thereby created what wasn't but what could have been and might yet be. No actuality for us, only potential.

The children and I were fugitives from consensual reality. We hiked or skied to arrive or paddled a canoe, a kayak or roared across the splendid lake in a battered motorboat.

There was at first no forest path. We made our way through brambles and weeds, past ancient trees, crystal brooks and muddy swamps while balancing on rotted logs and tripping on tangled roots and granite rock outcroppings.

Then, as in the land of Oz, the spectral tower rose before us, taller by far than the majestic trees and as just as remarkable.

Oh, to live ... beyond the treetops ... way up high ... over the rainbow ... and so on.

VI

Survival

Schizophrenia

A young man I know came down a few years ago with a case of schizophrenia. He had been a quiet, brainy sort, professorial, warm-hearted, modest, shuffling, preoccupied, tolerant and sloppy; argumentative, conversant in most matters; likable, tolerant; rational; an atheist, a liberal, a humanist.

What seemed sudden but probably took place over a long period of time, weeks or months, he became someone else, loud, angry, rambling, accusatory, pontifical. Whether with audience or not, he lectured on the evils of child sexual abuse.

Had he himself been abused? I don't know but think not.

Alarming was his life in the spectral world and the disturbing voices that he hears. He talks with God. "I am an Atheist," he said, "and yet I talk with God." Did he appreciate the humor?

God seems now to have faded. But the voices have not. They haunt him still; he finds them disturbing. They threaten to show him scenes of violent destruction and horror. Over the years he has come to understand them to be products of his own mind. But they remain intolerable.

He believes that his only way to silence them is to return to the hospital and have his medication adjusted. He does this at least once a month.

He is unhappy and despairing. He is hard to talk with. He is very withdrawn.

I am a psychologist … and I don't understand. What is the matter? What can be done?

He must feel trapped in a brain and a body that have been invaded by alien forces.

I don't know what to say when I am with him.

What has gone wrong?

Heredity? Schizophrenic genes? I have no idea. Perhaps he swallowed street drugs that paralyzed his mind.

He is hurting and no one can say why.

The experience of losing one's mind is bewildering, terrifying. It is possession by angry gods.

I have seen in Haiti Voundon ceremonies during which gods—*lwa-yo*—take over mind and body. The person, entranced, assumes the characteristics of the *lwa* to become a spirit.

That has happened to this young man.

He was mild-mannered. He is now aggressive and pontificating. He was gentle; approachable. He is now remote and intimidating.

He is a person possessed.

What is it subjectively to be possessed by an angry god? What does one imagine has become of one's self? There must be an immense sense of loss accompanied by an infusion of infernal power, immersed in a state of loss, of bewilderment.

Does one ask—what has become of me? Am I frightened? Am I other than who I am? Or or there only silence?

It is here that an old fashioned diagnostic assessment might for the suffering person come in handy. At the very least it could provide a sense of closure: "I came down with an illness that is called 'schizophrenia.'". Or, "This is not me. I am not this way. I have been on a bad trip."

Knowing no more than that it is a knowable condition may make it possible to imagine a cure, a return some day to the familiar self, perhaps even carrying along some of the positive qualities found while in that alternative universe but leaving behind the negative ones.

I may be a psychologist but I don't have a clue.

No one but he can hear his voices. They are very real to him although he also knows that they originate somewhere inside his head. They are annoying. They are insulting. He wishes he could shut them off but, try as he might, he cannot.

Perhaps if he were to enroll in an expressive arts group devoted to spontaneous writing, improv theater, expressive music or free-hand art. No need to be self-consciously therapeutic about this but the climate must surely be extremely supportive and, just as necessary—conversational; dialogic.

In such a group, he might be able to converse with the voices that haunt him and by so doing find himself able to control them, perhaps even to the extent of transforming them into art.

What I am proposing may not work.

By God! I wish the young man every success.

Derangement

When considering mental health and its promotion, it is best, I think, to take a broad, contextual view. Consider it theater. One is offered a most conventional cast, a therapist and a therapee both of whom appear on a stage which is the consulting room.

Who is the therapist? A friend? A relation? An actor? A random clown who happened by?

And what of the therapee? A person? A lonely person? A friendless person? A person seeking entertainment? Enrichment? Enlightenment? A person with a problem? A person confronted with a choice?

What is the significance of the room in which they meet? Why a room? Why not a hayfield? A skating rink? A mountain top? An outhouse? A clearing?

What are the rules, explicit or implied, that govern the interaction?

Are we not ham-strung by a world view that requires sanitation, precision and replicability nowhere more clearly experienced than at MacDonald's?

But the therapist/therapee unit must also be an alternative family, a floating family, a haven, a conversation, a birthplace; a home.

VII

Interim Summary

Yes, it is true: I have worked with kids ever since I, too, was a child, first at age thirteen as a camp counselor; later I taught swimming and boating at the New Jersey Camp for Blind Children. Later still as school psychologist, then as experimental educator, Community Mental Health Worker with children and youth from Boston and suburbs. Then as counselor way off the beaten track.

I have seen kids in Russia and Haiti, in court and school.

I have had kids of my own. And grandchildren. And chickens. And donkeys. And dogs.

... what have I taken from that?

Drama. It is now clear that drama is a necessary precondition to growth and development. Drama can be found everywhere, even at home. But it is harder to deal with there. The stage is too small.

I was fortunate. As a child, my parents enrolled me in progressive schools, Bank Street College's experimental kindergarten, then the City and Country School founded by one Caroline Pratt, a disciple of John Dewey; next, the Little Red Schoolhouse, founded by another Dewey disciple, Elisabeth Irwin.

It all occurred in Greenwich Village. Those schools all remain, none outmoded, quaint, antique but still relevant. All strong; all doing well. All influential.

The Little Red School House, the school I attended from age ten through high school, closed its doors each year at the end of May. Us kids—those whose parents agreed—were sent to an affiliated overnight camp for the entire month of June. "June

Camp." There was nothing exceptional about the program. It included standards like sports, hikes, stories around the campfire. But the experience was memorable. We found new worlds that we took for our own; we were no longer bound to our parents. We had were given a test flight from the nest after which we glided back on stronger wings.

Many of us were the only children in our families. I myself was. At most families produced two. ("It seemed wrong," my mother explained, "to bring Jewish children into a world that contained Hitler.") June Camp allowed us to develop relationships with our peers that approximated what others have with brothers and sisters.

June Camp, the *idea* of camp, remained with me. I became a carrier of the word and repeated it for subsequent generations ... as waterfront director at the New Jersey Camp for Blind Children where kids came from the depths of Princeton, Elizabeth and Newark. I taught them to swim.

Later, as a member of a university team, I helped plot a better Boston school system. As a step toward this accomplishment, we helped parents create a daycare center in the basement of a public housing project.

And we brought Boston children to the beach and to state parks where we sat by campfires and told stories and talked about everything and nothing in particular.

And in Russia and Haiti I visited programs, elements of which I thought might be replicated in the US. Homeless children in St. Petersburg were taken to art museums, concerts and circuses; a group home there had a touch of warmth, adventure and civility.

In Haiti, inspiration was found in community programs located in the mountains that brought children from Port-au-Prince to the country and mountain children to the city.

There was nothing conventionally therapeutic about any of this. But there was always an awareness of that we were in the presence of each other.

I had a growing epiphany: "Work with children is best done in a dark forest or an open field, by a flowing stream or while carried along by a breeze in a sailboat on a clear mountain lake."

That place in Vermont was my office. It was there that I immersed myself for many years. It was a good thing in itself but represented more, an ideal, approximated but seldom realized, yet it remains before my eyes even now, a vision of what might and ought to be.

Imitations of Immortality

Well ... it has been a life. A good life. Certainly not a bad one. The scars it has left have been few and far from pitiable. Anyway, I am now *en route* to salvation or ... not.

Much was learned along the way but I cannot remember what it was. The cop-out of old age is incapacity. The mind crumbles and recollections leak, despoiling the landscape.

The fifth essence of my accumulated wisdom is: God may exist. Evidence lies in the observable aesthetic sense in dogs.

When Milly, our current canine, lived with us at the Clearing, for example, she like Jenny, our preceding mutt, was given to sitting on the Consultation Rock admiring the exquisite scene before her, the lovely lake and the mountains beyond, for a long, long time. Perhaps it was the clouds or the ripples on the water that transfixed her. I do not know. I doubt that it was the ducks, the loons, the herons or the hawks. But whatever it was that held her attention was not the result of training. It was surely that Milly was entranced by beauty. I shared her assessment thus did we transcend our species.

How might this common response to nature's glory otherwise be explained? Why does a love of beauty exist anyway? Is esthetics a survival mechanism? In people? In dogs?

While we are on the subject: Dogs and people are not in a single hereditary line. That is, we are not descended from dogs nor they from us. Yet their minds and bodies are oddly similar to our own.

That is, they have eyes in the front of their heads that allow for binocular vision. They have lungs, stomachs, arms, legs and joints that are homologous to ours. They strive to be good. And, as I wrote, they appreciate beauty. But we are not close relatives.

What if we looked to more distant species? What might we have in common? There is an infinitude, after all, of other life forms from which we might have descended. Insects are organized different than we are as are octopi who, I understand, are considerably more intelligent than they appear. Do we share features and mind-sets with bizarre creatures such as these?

Life forms vary. There are many threads, ours and that of the dogs having been the present focus. But the earth might as easily have been dominated by forms as unlike us as crustaceans and worms.

It is as if some inexplicable force were experimenting: Trying this pattern on a bunch of animals and trying that one on others. And why not? So ... how to explain *similarities* of body and mind, not differences? How did the stomach, the heart, the liver and skin, the aesthetic and morality of a dog so closely resemble our own if there was no historic relation between us? How much are we like the worm?

Similarities within a species are understandable. It is not surprising that all primates have pretty much the same bodies and brains. But— taking a step back—primates and canines? That is another matter altogether. Why do they have similar structures?

So: Why do dogs and humans agree on matters of natural beauty? Answer: Esthetics must be related across species for survival.

God has been messing around, experimenting with a variety of models.

The god that I have in mind is not bearded and is neither a man nor a woman, a dog nor a cat nor a cockroach. ... It is probably an entity entirely unrecognizable by the likes of us. It may, for example, resemble a deer tic.

VIII

A Brief Intermission

Dear Editor,

Just before my wife and I moved into the Kendal retirement community, our younger granddaughter was busy selecting a college. "Go to Dartmouth!" we begged. "It's right down the road." Expectations high, she signed up for a tour of the campus. But she returned an hour or so later looking glum. "This is definitely not the place for me," she said. "The emphasis," she explained, "is on fraternities, sororities, sports and parties."

A couple of years later, a Russian friend, an undergraduate at a prestigious Moscow Institute, visited us. She took the same tour. I accompanied her as surrogate grandparent. Walking backward, the guide told of the happy life of the Dartmouth student. Good courses to be sure but lots of time for making whoopie.

"I can't believe this," the Russian student said afterward. "Is this really one of the best universities in the United States?"

"It is," I explained sheepishly. "It just has a peculiar way of selling itself. Education is a business, you see."

She did not see.

I cannot help but suspect that these tales of woe are related to the campus culture that was examined recently at the current Dartmouth rape trial.

Sincerely,

Milly's Morning

Wednesday morning. Nine o'clock. Milly and I strolled along the paths in the empty field adjacent to Kendal, our lovely Geezer Ghetto. There she met her dear friend, Squirt. They chased each other. And both pooped.

Then we returned to the apartment.

I went to the clinic to see what could be done about the wax in my ears, particularly the right one. Stella, the nurse, peered in via her cold, silver-toned flashlight. "Lots of wax there," she said referring to the right ear. She looked into the left one. "A lot in there, too," she said. "But less." She advised me to drip salad oil in each ear before bedtime. "Any oil will do except machine oil."

I am sitting now in Kendal's "Common Room" waiting to meet Eliot, the chair of PIG, our Photography Interest Group. I am in charge of taking pictures of new residents. But am about to quit. Too hard to track them down; too formal. I do love snapping pictures but prefer to do so on the sly. Maybe I can find someone else to take on the formal portrait assignment. We'll see what Eliot thinks.

I am backing off lots of things these days. Mary and I are co-chairs of the Events Committee, a key responsibility. We haul old friends in from previous lives. They tell the assembled multitude about interesting things that they are doing, have done or may do. And we encourage residents to make presentations as well of whatever they wish, musical events, art, theater, literature, peace, justice, past lives and professions.

The entire institution is a stage from which one may amuse and educate the entire Kendal population.

But it takes time to arrange these things. Much busy work is involved, like running a booking agency. We have been at it for two years now. And I have promises to keep ... and a pile of stuff to do before I sleep.

Friends walk by some with walkers, some with canes, some on legs, steady or otherwise. They wave and say, "hi."

An email from Bill, director of the Unadilla Theater down the road: "Probably a lost cause, but we are doing Uncle Vanya again. I hear Waffles calling? Will you play that part again? Please."

I write back that I am happy to be asked but am too damned busy.

"Busy"? Doing *what* for God's sake?

Writing a memoir.

IX

Utopia

I have always enjoyed the bucolic but never in its particulars nor as woodsman or gardener, only as romantic. I seldom dirty my hands; I can't identify much flora and pay little attention to fauna except to exclaim, "Looka the rabbit!" or "Wow! Lotta of birds this morning!" Physical exertion is confined to snoozing in the sun, picking wild berries or walking with Milly to the lake. It was always thus.

Although a city boy, I found myself early on drawn to the *Gemütlichkeit* of the country, the meditative quiet, the drowsy cousin to the screeching city. It was a spiritual matter.

It was also political. Progressive education had romantic roots in the silvan as did revolutionary movements of past eras ... Rousseauvian romantics, Tolstovians, Ghandians, Boy and Girl Scouts, Wanderfolgen, and Komsomolskaya Youth.

Fresh air fetish came with the Industrial Revolution. Bank Street College of Education's experimental preschool made little kids take their daily naps in open air window boxes even during the winter. The Shady Hill School in Cambridge, Massachusetts, provided no heat in its classrooms.

From ages six through nine, I attended the City and Country School in New York so named because children were brought on visits to the forests, fields and farms.

And the Little Red School House closed its doors during the month of June. Students then embarked to "June Camp" where we breathed the good and pleasant air, swam, played ball, sang folk songs, read stories, made innocent mischief, and felt more independent than we were.

The Clearing

The Clearing has been my baby. I conceived it, bore it, cradled it, nurtured it, sent it off to school and on its way. It is now grown and I am old and each of us have our destinies to follow. We hope that the place will be purchased by an idealistic foster couple who will love it as we have.

"No need to sell at all," I tell myself ... better to myself than to Mary who would instantly remind me of obvious truth which is right there in front of my nose: We are ready to move on.

I prefer fiction to truth, the fiction that the Clearing represents a point of view, a philosophy, a way of life; a cure for what ails you. It represents a reasonable way of thinking about deviance and life: Ignore diagnosis and think instead ... ambiance, situation, space, relation, theater, poetry, architecture, dance, music, art, and justice.

Okay. I know. I know. I can see it in that look on your face. But hold on. Listen. Give me a moment and I shall explain. That, after all, is what this book is about.

Explain? No. I shall lay it out instead. I shall create a tale of a simpler and more sensible way of thinking ... about unhappiness in human affairs. And I shall offer instructions on how precisely to proceed into that storied realm of true happiness, Eden, the garden of danger and delight. But first, the axioms that undergird our thinking:

Axiom #1: Ain't nobody sick unless a bug can be found.

Axiom #2: Everything consequential is situational.

Axiom #3: The Revolution is won.

Wow

Remember the Skazka, a little Russian restaurant on Barrow Street? Bobby Nemiroff's parents ran it. Bobby later married Lorraine Hansbury, author of "Raison in the Sun." Bobby's dad kept a copy of the 1936 Soviet constitution in the restaurant behind the cash register. He showed it to my parents and me one evening with the comment:

"This is the most democratic constitution in the world."

"Wow," I thought. "Oh Wow."

A Geezer in a Ghetto

I am in a selfish frame of mind and do not have within me the considerable effort required to focus on the proposed expansion of Kendal, our retirement community. Neither am I convinced that I have a dog in that fight anyway. When the dust settles and the doors of the new facility swing open to new residents, my ashes, lovingly admixed with Mary's, will have long since been scattered to the winds.

I plan instead to spend the remainder of my dotage unearthing sense in my previous life, the one when I lived in the real world. I intend to do so by writing, gazing at the stars, and strolling along with young Milly after which I shall eat, sleep, gaze on grandchildren in full bloom, travel some, and indulge in social action on behalf of good people in some distant country, Haiti perhaps, Palestine or Ukraine.

Everything else is a distraction, meetings especially, interminable meetings that deal exclusively with the soporific ....

Yes, Management wants Kendal to expand. For the most part, we, the Residents, wish the place to remain unchanged. Management wins because new customers are always required; they arrive with entrance fees in hand, hard cash essential to paying the bills.

The model is one of infinite growth. Entrance fees will always be needed and when will it end? When markets collapse, when competitive pastures appear. The model is an inherently unstable one ... about which I know nothing and have nothing to say.

I myself choose to walk a different path, one that leads only to a sense of community, a community in which each person's needs and agendas are celebrated, nurtured to become the subjects of stimulating conversation and where growth takes place naturally as a function of multiple, sparkling and inchoate possibilities.

Size alone is not a critical factor. How we relate to one another and to our selves is the nub of the matter. We get along very well here at Kendal. It is our spirit that makes this a fine place to live. That spirit needs always to be nurtured and in so doing we approach the goals that we have set for ourselves.

"Ambience" is always the watchword.

Fraud

I am a fraud. I am a fraud because I accept payment because people have been led to believe that by virtue of a paper from some damned institution of higher learning attesting to my virtues, the words that I utter, the smiles and the gestures, the grunts, the burps and the shouts, contain the power of sorcery, a witch's brew of powers that banish unhappiness.

Oh, yes: I am a fraud.

Yet beneficial effects are often attested to following our mere sharing of time and space. Such phenomena are worth examining.

Theater comes to mind. The Clearing is a stage. We act. We create a situation that creates positive challenges to our behavior and obliges us to respond in new and unaccustomed ways to signals from others. Thus we learn of our potential to be unlike what we had always assumed that we were.

This occurs most reliably, I suspect, when we find ourselves in new places and meet new people in unpracticed interactions. Our responses require us to call forth hidden—often pleasing but occasionally unpleasant—selves. Or to create one or the other on the spot.

To the extent that I have provided kids with a stage and a situation, I might not have been much of a fraud after all but rather a genial if bumbling host.

The Clearing's End

It is said that one must begin at the beginning. I shall start at the end.

We are selling the Clearing. We have owned it for some forty-two years and have had one building or another in place for about forty. Three incarnations all told. Many good times were had and it was here that I played with children full time for fifteen years and way more part time.

I will miss the place. Sure. Regrets about selling it? Yes and no. But sell it we must. We are elders you see, Mary and I, too creaky to frolic, too decayed to delight in the place as it deserves to be delighted in and certainly too far gone to keep up with occasional maintenance.

We have tried to interest educational outfits in taking it over but without success.

If only we had a grandchild or two who was in a position to use it, we would happily turn it over to him or to her. But they are all young adults now, straining to make their ways in the world and have no time to be distracted by their grandparents' foolish zeal. I use the word, "foolish" only in reference to the ten to fifteen thousand dollars a year that it costs to maintain the place. That's a lot of money. Think of all of the good fun one can have for such hard-earned *dinero*.

Advanced age is regrettable. Worse is illness, death and the evaporation of once valued traces. Most terrible of all is lethargy. Yet what a splendid mountaintop view age offers us! From there we may observe and ponder that vast panorama of our lives. Transposing even a tiny portion of it into words is an arduous task but one that may eventually be seen by archivists as having been worth the effort.

Family

The theory—if I may be so bold—of mental health to which I adhere, has it that life is all about affiliation centered on the creation of an ersatz, theatrically enhanced, temporary family against which the family of origin may resonate and be judged.

What does that imply for the therapist who presides? What of his or her own family, the one apart from fiction, the one that is constituted of flesh, blood, and a history; a spouse and children, and all the inevitable complexities?

Our Brave Band

Re: Our sixty-fifth high school class reunion ...

Dear Vic.

Thank you for your note.

Our class must have been for you as it was for me—and the rest of us—a kind of extended family. Everyone was either a single child or at most had one sibling. In your case you were fortunate to have had a terrific sister. But Greta, eleven years your junior, seemed almost to have been part of another generation.

And so you and I and all the rest of us turned to each other. We became the brothers and sisters that our human species has evolved to require.

Each of us played a role in that *ersatz* family. Your role as I experienced it might be described as the Huck Finn, the proto-hippy, the guy given to unlikely adventures thus to open all of us to worlds beyond what we had imagined existed.

These, as I saw them, were in three domains that resonated well in the early adolescent: The Great Outdoors, Sex, and Music (not necessarily in that order).

The sex and the music I leave for others to discuss. But I want to state here and now that your fascination with and knowledge of the outdoors influenced me greatly. Your parents' resort camps for grownups offered a world unlike any that I had experienced or imagined.

Even as a kid, your own role in running these places was central. I was impressed that you—a city kid—had extensive knowledge of the forests, the flora and the fauna, and could do hands-on work, and could assume the accompanying responsibilities.

I know that these images became prototypes for the lives in Vermont that Mary and I lived so many years later.

Enough, brother. The day is dawning. I am off to the Clearing to meet the gas man for one final time.

We look forward to seeing you at our next gathering of alums.

Bob

Walks Per Day

Milly and I walk together three, sometimes four, times a day. We often go by the river here at Kendal along the steep, switch-back trail reputedly dangerous for old folks or we cut through the bushes to the deteriorating sidewalk on the neighboring land where once there were houses but now there is only pavement and grasses grown untended.

Milly is a reasonable dog, one might even say a civilized dog. We do not train her in the ordinary sense. We communicate mysteriously, possibly through telepathy. She adheres to proper behavior on her own with no instruction from me. For example, she always finds a discrete spot well off the path upon which to deposit her poop. I do not need to carry a pooper-scooper or, worse, a little plastic bag of the sort I rail against because the environment is surely far more poorly served by plastic than it is by uncollected dog poop.

Milly greets her canine friends as well as the people she knows—and even those she doesn't—in a most cheerful manner, neither subservient nor threatening. This miraculously triggers similar behavior in others—even the worst of them. Aloof people smile. Bad dogs wag their tails, and dance around her. Frightened children giggle and screech with delight.

She is the most civilized dog I have known. But she didn't learn any of it from me.

No Rabbi

Let's get something straight. I am your MC for the evening, not your Rabbi. I would indeed make a most unconventional, highly unlikely excuse for a Rabbi. I am an atheist. My parents and some of my grandparents were atheists, too. I never even had a *bar mitzvah.*

Yet I am Jewish. Proudly so. A person may say, "I used to be Catholic" or "I am a lapsed Episcopalian" or "When I was a child I was a Voudonisan."

Not so with Jews. Once a Jew, always a Jew, theology notwithstanding. It is in the blood, in the phrasing of the language, in the habit of the mind. A lapse is impossible.

I have something of an understanding of this and shall do my best to explain it to you with particular reference to Rosh Hashanah.

To begin with, Judaism is dialectical in nature. Its theology is argumentative, replete with reasonable compromise. Take the story of Abraham and Isaac. God, in an apparent fit of personal insecurity, asks Abraham to demonstrate his piety by sacrificing his only son, Isaac. Abraham is understandably reluctant to commit this awful act so God compromises and accepts the slaughter of a lamb instead.

The episode is a dramatic haggle: God demands; Abraham answers in the negative; God gives ground much to the satisfaction of both Abraham and Him/Her self thus resolving the matter with civility.

Thesis, Antithesis, Synthesis.

Judaism promotes an argumentative habit of mind; a dialog.

One may see illustrations in the works of such famous Jewish atheists as Marx, Freud, and Einstein: Capital and Labor resolved in Socialism; Id and Superego resolved in Ego; light as ray versus light as photon resolved in an inexplicable alternation between the two.

So it is in Jewish theology. God commands; the human person presents a counter offer. In the end, something gets worked out.

This is the habit of thought of the Middle East merchant. "How much do you want for that bauble?" "Ten dollars." "I'll give you seven-fifty." "Eight and a quarter and it's yours."

It is also the habit of the courtroom. What is your plea?

"Innocent."

"Guilty: Thirty days."

"Extenuating Circumstances!"

"So, all right. Ten days."

Rosh Hashanah is a holiday of score-keeping, of determining culpability, of assigning terms of repayment. All of this results, hopefully, in redemption, a reprieve from damnation. The drama occurs in a back-and-forth in which the conflict between God's law and the failings of the human person is debated while at the same time inventory is taken, and we measure where we stand as in the time of harvest when we size up the granary.

But what seems to me distinctively Jewish about the Rosh Hashanah staging is that the deity and the human being appear on a refreshingly equal level. The human being, man or woman, speaks freely with God, who receives pleas as well as angry accusations.

Of note is that Rosh Hashanah occurs in the autumn at the time of harvest. "Let us assess what we have. Is there enough to last the winter or will we suffer?"

The harvest reaped is ethical behavior. "Have I been a good person or have I omitted something or forgotten someone or left somewhere an unpaid debt of insult, dishonesty or cruelty?"

The stage of this Rosh Hashanah theater, the ritual meal, is where we examine our hidden soul to find, before God's eye spots it, where we are lacking, where debts remain to be paid.

For each debt, for each transgression, repentance is dramatized by tossing a straw into a body of water accompanied by a prayer of repentance. The feast ends with the sounding of the horn, the *shofar*, that announces the coming of God to render heavenly justice.

God renders such judgment ten days later at Yom Kippur. The appellant meanwhile attempts to make amends to everyone he or she has wronged during the previous year or to whom debts remain outstanding, and endeavors to expiate all sins and to come up with what is due. God is informed of these efforts as part of the negotiation.

Rosh Hashanah is thus a drama of resolution familiar to anyone who has had to deal with the IRS.

But among us Jews the currency is not cash so much as decency. The question to be asked is: Have I been a good person?

★★★★

It is said that Jews are God's chosen people. Does that mean that He (or She) favors them over all others? That is perhaps an early reading. But more likely is the view that God demands more of Jews than of anyone. He/She has anointed Jews to be His/Her emissaries to bring the light of ethical behavior to everyone in the world.

Yahweh, the Jewish god, was once a mere village deity, small and parochial. The contribution of Judaism was to envision a universal force, a God for all of humanity, indeed for all of life.

It is because of this ethically-oriented theology that we today see so many Jewish do-gooders, people committed to justice, to civil rights, to equality, to democracy, and indeed to democratic socialism.

Such preoccupations have made Jews more unpopular than ever with the bigots and tyrants of our time even those with whom Judaism is nominally shared ... such as many of our brothers and sisters in Israel.

The Loss of Paradise

We sold the Clearing last month. Very Big Deal. We've owned it for forty-two years depending on how you count.

It was acquired in three purchases, the first was a long time ago, 1972. It was nothing but forest then, woods, mud, rocks, flora and fauna. We built houses on it over time, not homes but rather containers of a poorly articulated yet powerful utopian vision wrapped in a mantle of mental health.

What did I who was born and nurtured in Manhattan know about such a wild and savage place? Precious little.

I had a hunch, an unexamined predilection that grew from knowing children at camps and on the streets of Boston and Newton.

It was a vision, one might call it that, not a particularly mystical one but rather a dreamy accompaniment to workaday life that entered my brain through monotonous conversations and unremarkable observations.

The implicit assumption: The job of camp-type counselor is to create a situation in which a kid might find a way to know his or her otherwise unknowable soul in intimate commerce with other unknowable souls, a state of things normally a matter of mystery, well beyond awareness and usually thought of as more in the realm of mysticism. Thus we knowingly chuckle because we are rational people.

But by living with others and sharing time and space, a sense of who one is or may eventually become is formed and emerges, seldom beckoned by anybody's will but because, simply because, given how things are, that's the way the ball bounces.

The child progresses in his or her circumstances—whether familial or social—from unknown-new-kid to an increasingly realized individual with unmistakeable characteristics—positive or otherwise. He or she becomes the repository of consensually acknowledged attributes, "good at sports," "jerk," "funny," "dweeb," "great to hang out with."

These are for the most part newly attached labels possibly different at school than those attributed at home where he or she might be known merely as "cute," "mischievous," "good," "bad," or, worse, "invisible."

It is the movement toward recognition and visibility that becomes the road to individuation and maturity. Is it not?

And what does any of this have to do with the land we sold?

I intend to make all this perfectly clear ... eventually .... Or not.

Priut Almus

Priut Almus is—or was—a magically innovative children's shelter in St. Petersburg, Russia. It is an example of what I am calling a "transitional" institution and my sense of what is needed here in the US and elsewhere. It is a homey place.

I visited for a few days to a couple of weeks annually for a period of about a half dozen years and found a role for myself as the house grandfather. *"Dye-dye Bob,"* they called me, "Grandpa Bob."

"Priut" means "shelter" in Russian. "Almus" is a town in Crimea where the shelter children once spent a particularly good summer in the early days of the institution and thought it would make a good name for the place they loved.

I ring the bell. Sergei unlocks the door and lets me in. He is a tall, middle-aged fellow with a grizzled incipient beard. *"Priviet,"* he says—"Hi." He smiles while locking the door behind me. It is poorly lit inside but not quite shabby. Snowsuits are arranged more or less neatly on hooks and boots are lying about on the floor in some attempt at order. A flight of stairs is on the right. There are clumping sounds and the laughter and squeals of children racing the corridor on the floor above. I climb the stairs. Children rush me. They hug me. We have not seen each other in a year. Staff members, two women and a man, stand by grinning. I am part of a family.

As in other Russian children's shelters, residents come and go. By regional law, no child can remain in Almus for more than one year. It is expected that by then he or she will be returned home, living in an orphanage or adopted. Admission to the priut requires neither court proceedings nor loss of parental custody. Although some children are brought in by the police, some are brought by their parents and others simply knock on the door and request admission on their own. The procedure is remarkably informal in view of the rule-bound nature of Russian civic society.

Priutye (plural of "*priut*") did not exist during Soviet times but were abundant in the Tsarist eras. It reappeared with the demise of the Soviet regime.

"I *love* Almus," a kid whose family had been homeless told me. "But my mom found an apartment for us and I think we will be okay."

A cheerful little girl explained, "I am here because my mom had an operation. She will be out of the hospital in a week and then I will go back home. But we live just down the street so I will go to Almus for after-school games, art and stuff whenever I feel like it."

A fourteen year old boy told me about his father's alcoholism and violence. "I don't want to go home. If I see my dad again, I will kill him. If they put me in an orphanage, I will run away. I don't care."

Almus is an active, warm, mostly happy place. It is a community center, social service agency and short term residence wrapped up into one. There is a strong element of the arts that permeates the program: painting, music, trips to museums and the circus.

The founder/director Mikhail Makarovitch—"*Makarich*"—was raised in an orphanage during WWII. He felt abandoned and powerless. He survived, he explains, by hanging around the Leningrad Children's Theater. It became an alternative family to him. He worked on sets, became stage manager and eventually actor and director. That was his career. He started Almus to give children in need a similar alternative setting, imaginative and responsive to their needs.

But his vision proved a bit radical for the local bureaucracy. Makarich fought to allow children to stay for longer than the mandated one year limit if they needed to. He argued well with the fury and dramatic flair learned from his years in the theater fueled by angry memories of his own years in an orphanage. Although he often won the battles and was widely respected, he made powerful enemies. He was forced out in 2008.[8]

---

[8] A more complete discussion of Priut Almus may be found in my book, "Tales of Priut Almus," iUniverse, 2009

X

Family Courts

Guardians ad Litem

Once retired, I became a "Guardian ad Litem," a part-time volunteer advocate for children in Vermont's juvenile and family courts, a worthwhile endeavor. I did that for about eight years.

When a person, child or adult, thinks "court" what comes to mind? A fortress? A palace? A police station? A prison? And lawyers? Be wary of lawyers. Watch your step. They talk fast and their words have powers. If you garble what you say or get it wrong, you are done for. Lawyers are dangerous.

The judge? Dressed in black like a high priest, he or she sits behind an alter and reads from papers that contain your secrets. You cannot hide from the judge. The judge sees your sins. The judge inflicts punishment. The judge is Oz, Great and Terrible. And you are Dorothy. The judge is awesome. You are awed.

Question: Can we generate a more felicitous popular perception of court? Is it possible to view it as a benevolent place, a respite from meanness and stupidity, an eden of understanding and equanimity?

For felicitous perceptions to take root, they must be nurtured in experience. The court's client, whether adult or child, must leave each session with a sense that he or she has been fully heard and seen.

It is the same whether for child or adult.

The means to achieve trust in legal theater varies from individual to individual according to his or her prior experiences and developmental level. And if a person has the sense of being seen and heard, "winning" the case may become less important than the perception that the process has been a fair one.

But it is often not simple.

A twelve year old girl, an iconic composite of several children I have known, informed me with characteristic imperiousness that she wants her sensitive, alcoholic, non custodial mother to take charge of her because her father, although having a good enough job, an okay home and a sympathetic new wife, is "mean." It was father who had initiated the separation that led to the divorce.

I met with father. He impressed me as a bright well spoken fellow. He was surprised by his daughter's allegation. "We get along very well," he said providing credible anecdotes about all they do together, the things they talk about, her cuddling up next to him as they watch television together and so on.

I told the girl when I next saw her that her father was not aware that they have a problem. "That's so typical of him," she growled, "an example of what I am up against. He never has a clue about anything."

"Does he abuse you?" I wondered, offering a few, cautious examples.

"Oh, no!" she said. "No way. I just call him 'mean' because he takes away my computer for no reason, grounds me even though I never do anything wrong and wont let me visit my friends even when all we do is our homework together. He is a pain in the butt."

A hearing was coming up but a change in the custody arrangement did not appear in the cards as far as the court was concerned.

"I want to testify," the girl said. "I insist on my right to do so!"

"Against your *father*?" I asked.

"Yes," she said with a chill in her voice.

As an old shrink, I understood perfectly. The girl had identified with the rejected mother. Her motive was not at issue, neither was the substance of her allegations. But the court's respect for her point of view was.

Exactly where might the best interests of such a kid lie? In her stated wish to be "divorced" from father as was her mother and identified with her in banishment and self-pity? Or in her present Eden where she has replaced mother in what might well be a tangled oedipal nightmare?

Who is to say? But at the very least, the court may prove of use by offering the girl the services of an elder with an unbiased eye and an acutely sensitive ear. Though there may be no easy answer, the girl would surely benefit from society's judgement unsullied by reproach and based on her voice being heard; sometimes even the reverberating echoes beyond what she intended to say.

Her case is like many others involving children in that there is no perfect resolution, no perpetrator and no victim; no one at fault. The issue is not crime but human relations.

The court is not a mental health clinic nor ought it be. It is an institution designed to allocate culpability and in so doing presumes a zero-sum game, not a useful paradigm in child development. The girl and her family might have been better served by a canny mediator able to sort out the needs of all parties while leading them to consider a solution minimizing acrimony and maximizing civilized behavior and discourse.

Typically each parent arrives in court with a fixed position often with an attorney in tow who serves as a megaphone to amplify his or her injured voice.

The child by the time of the hearing has become the dead horse on the living room floor, the central figure whose overwhelming presence is willfully ignored. Faced with divorced parents intent on doing each other harm and with neither the interest nor the capacity to take notice, the child is at risk of falling into an abyss of cynicism.

A remedy can be a sympathetic judge, attorneys who see their task as something greater than winning points, ancillary court personnel - including GALS - who are easy to talk with and a court atmosphere that is at once businesslike and convivial. The court may become a venue where even unspoken cries are heard, the center of a tribal community where elders, concerned with the welfare of everyone, see and hear the worst and the best with equanimity thus to maintain a delicate balance in all things.

The approach I am recommending is neither new nor utopian. It is already practiced in many of our courtrooms. I know judges who spend hours the night before a case is scheduled reading all the stories, absorbing their details and import. On the following morning the hearing opens with a hearty, "Hello, Billy! How are you doing? I understand that you had a ball game yesterday. How did it go?"

With a judge like that presiding, the child's age recedes as a critical factor as does his or her particular history of trauma, abuse or neither. The judge has clarified something essential and reassuring about what can be expected from the ensuing theatrical event.

In the years that I have known them, the Vermont Family and Juvenile Courts have come a long way toward providing a felicitous yet reassuringly professional venue. I am confident that they have it within them to do even better in the future.

A Family

Social Services decided upon thorough investigation that two little girls were being served poorly by their parents who surely were having a rough time of it. They were living on welfare, the children came to school unclean and poorly clothed. There was suspicion of substance abuse.

This was a New Hampshire Family Court. I was appointed child guardian. My job was to advise the judge on the best outcome from the point of view of the child's developmental needs.

I visited the home several times. Although the mood was depressed and the scene chaotic—far from ideal—there were positive aspects. Attachment of child-to-parent was evident. Mother and father watched the children at play in the yard, cautioned them when it seemed that there was a need to do so and called them in for lunch. They loved their children.

At school, the girls were marginal to the group but not entirely removed from it. They were not as well dressed as the other children and did not interact much with them. I thought that the teachers did not make sufficient efforts to include them.

The children, though they seemed bright enough, were only marginal students. They felt excluded and were reluctant to attend.

The State had tried for several years to remove them from the home and to place them in foster care.

I was new to the scene, replacing a previous guardian. My knee-jerk bias is to oppose foster care. I have two reasons. First, a good foster home—especially for a needy child—is a rare find anywhere. Second, giving up on a family sets a pattern of defeat that can continue down many generations.

Better, I thought, is a temporary reprise, an auxiliary family, a back-up, a retreat, a boarding school, a center in which sharing with the family of origin and support might occur naturally and as needed. Models in my mind included Priut Almus and, of course, the Clearing.

It happened that there was indeed such a place but it was outside of the purview of the New Hampshire Social Services. It was the foundation-sponsored boarding school, the Kurn Hattin Home. I had positive experience with the place some years previously. It was free and did not take children in state custody. Instead it was conceived as an alternative to foster care thus allowing parents to retain their rights. Its aim was to strengthen the family by working closely with all members during the child's stay, encouraging parent visitation and offering them considerable support and consultation. It prepares for reunification.

I suggested Kurn Hattin to the state social worker as an option worth exploring. But she handily turned it down, and, I thought, with entirely unjustified contempt.

A custody hearing was coming up in a few days. I suggested to the parents that they visit Kurn Hattin at once while they still had authority in the matter and to bring the kids with them to see what they thought.

The parents bought my idea.

The family had no car. Neither had they a friend prepared to drive them.

I knew that in my guardian role I was not permitted to drive clients but, given the situation and having nothing to lose except my volunteer position, I took the risk and volunteered to be their chauffeur.

The family loved what they saw of Kurn Hattin. The kids were ecstatic—especially after they saw the horses!

I told the girls that it might be a good idea to hold off discussing our adventures with their teachers until things were set.

But the social worker got the word, the state kicked me off the case, terminated parental rights, took custody of the children and placed them in foster care.

The parents were devastated.

I do not know what the children thought of all this.

XI

Models of Who We Are and Become

Heron

A perceptive friend, upon reading an early draft of these memoirs, came up with the following critique:

"The reader has no idea what you look like. You should describe yourself. You are a tall, thinnish guy with long legs that allow you to take two or more steps to every one of most people."

Okay. Here it is: I am a tall, thinnish old guy with long legs. I resemble a Great Blue Heron, this impression belied only by my unkempt grey hair and mustache. I tend to amble along while appearing to be lost in thought but in fact am more likely to be day-dreaming about lunch. Long legs allow for my casual stroll to equal the stride of conventionally-limbed companions.

Pastured

Is it reasonable to be concerned? ...

That our retirement community will lose its direction, its moral purpose, its social goal, its focus which is to enhance a person's farewell years. This is not simply a business. It is, dammit, a social service organization, hopefully so excellent as to be a public health model for the nation. As such, an exemplary balance sheet ought not be the goal, rather the mental and physical health of participants.

It has been the latter way pretty much. But now there is talk of expansion.

Keep your eye on the ball, I say. That suggests:

Diversity: The resident population must approximate the population at large; diversity along such dimensions as cultural, occupational, ethnic, racial, and economic.

It is, among other virtues, the radical social mission of our community that attracted Mary and me here. And many others, too.

Although the place offers little in the way of racial diversity, community members do in fact represent a fairly wide swath of occupations from teachers, social workers, ministers and librarians to leaders of business and government.

What concerns me is that with the understandable focus on our balance sheet, we will shortly price ourselves out of the middle class market—if we haven't already. The result will be an institution less interesting, more conventional and, from the point of view of the larger world, declining utility.

We are a 501(c)3 non profit corporation right up there with schools, universities, museums, hospitals, public broadcasting and libraries. None of them survive on fee-for-service income. All depend on supplementary funding whether through grants or taxes.

Why not us?

Here is what we face: A contemplated thirty new apartments reputedly to go for an entry fee of well over a half million dollars while the rest of us will be burdened by a monthly fee hike well ahead of the cost of living index.

I say: Take our mission seriously and bravely move toward social diversity, preserving meanwhile as much economic diversity as possible.

The risk of not doing so is to lose our high morale, our élan and our voice, and to become—a plain vanilla institution a condition bound, among other things, to have an eventual downside effect on recruitment and thus, paradoxically, our vaunted bottom line.

The Clearing

When we create the alternative, transitional, magical, reparative family we have been suggesting, we also make problems especially if the family of origin is weak, abusive, poverty-stricken or unstable as is true of most kids sent to the Clearing or, indeed, to any counselor.

The child, needy and stressed is offered calm, abundance and at least the appearance of understanding and acceptance. The therapist/host becomes parent surrogate *de facto*.

This is a situation fraught with danger. The setting has been created as a way-station on the road to maturity, not a substitute for the original family but rather part of a plan for its strengthening. The counseling venue, whether conventional or the Clearing, should be an island of calm, a place for gaining perspective and strength, a play-house, a theater, a sanctuary—not an alternative family.

The therapist/host must play it warm-hearted and cool; very, very cool indeed. In the paradigm suggested here, that person is neither doctor nor parent, nor even long term friend. He or she is simply a host, kindly but ephemeral, a facilitator rather than in charge, a friendly, familial sort but neither actually friend nor family. I see myself as theater director or camp counselor, minister or MC; *maître d'*.

I make it a point to avoid even being imagined as a physician because that suggests someone with a less than helpful magic, access to medicines, surgery and other such powers requiring merely passive accidence on the part of the patient.

Sometimes when we first meet, children call me, "Doctor."

"Whoa! I am in command of a fleet of boats here, a canoe, two kayaks and a sailing dingy," I explain. "You may call me "Captain Bob."

97

There are many social roles that carry my meaning. But, in addition to "doctor," the one that needs most to be shunned is "parent." Competition with the sending family is to be avoided at all costs.

This advice must be followed even when dealing with a marginal or inadequate family, biological or foster. Then, the host becomes a professional however informally attired, someone to help work things out often in concert with other professionals. But, again, as *facilitator*, not substitute for family head.

Part of the problem is of course the impossibility of long term continual, as distinct from transient, commitment. Counselors work with people in crisis and, although sometimes do so for months or even years, this is hardly comparable to the morass that is endemic even in marginally functioning families where it may last a lifetime.

As Captain Bob, I cannot advertise a lifetime commitment to a particular child. I have my own children, my own family; we have had a long history together. In contrast my relationship to the kid at the Clearing is studied, instrumental and transitional. It may be intense, memorable and even helpful but, among other things, it is only instrumental. That is, rather than a naturally evolving friendship, our being together has the specific purpose of triggering a process that will continue not with me but in other, more natural relationships.

Although the kid in question and I usually enjoy each other's company and look forward to the time we spend together, it is clear that I am not about to adopt him or her nor, if things go as they should, am I the focus of our relationship. I am merely the designer of the setting where the door is open to something good.

There are limits to the informal style that I advocate.

But kids do meet each other at the Clearing and sometimes long term, genuine relationships occur among them.

Disbelief

Let me put it this way: From the vantage point of public policy, what is the sensible thing to do with all those children for whom there is nothing? I mean kids from families that can't provide a home, kids who are abandoned, neglected, exploited, abused, starved or merely disliked? That comprises a lot of kids. Most societal solutions have little or no positive effect from the point of view either of the child, the family or the world at large. One might say that an inadequate solution is no solution at all having the probable long term result of exacerbating the problem rather than reducing it.

A child raised in a poorly functioning home has neither the resources, the mental strength nor the vision sufficient to imagine, let alone to construct, a better one.

The common solution arising from the adult gut of good will is adoption: simply to stick the child in a new and, hopefully, better home. But this often carries with it new problems. An abused or neglected child may not be able to adjust to a new, more favorable environment. He or she may, however perversely, test the new family to provoke a return to the former, accustomed although less favorable conditions. A battle may ensue with the foster or adoptive family in which the child loses—even if he or she wins.

In addition, there may be certain actual advantages, invisible to most reasonable people, to living not in a home at all but rather in an institution. The most important of these is the presence of a peer group.

A Russian girl I knew when she was five, a year before her adoption by a single, suburban American woman, returned with her new mother seven years later to visit the boarding school, the "*internat*," where she had lived. Many of the children were in fact orphans or came from abusive or alcoholic homes.

Her friends remembered her well and welcomed her with great warmth and excitement.

"You are *so* lucky," one girl said. "Now you have a mother!"

"Well," the adopted girl replied, "in some ways it is great in America. But in some ways I miss it here. My mom and I live out in the suburbs. It is just the two of us and it can get really boring. And sometimes my mom can be a pain.

"You kids have each other. It's like a big family here. You have friends around all the time. It is like camp. I miss it … in a way."

The orphan children stared at her in disbelief.

XII

Instrumentality

Grandma's House

A variety of hardware is available for repairing and remodeling human lives:

- The Counselor. This is someone who hears one, assesses the story and recommends a better course of action.
- The Psychotherapist. Following Freud, the therapist encourages regression to an infantile state then assists the patient in constructing a new, more functional way of being.
- Rewards. Reinforcers, negative or positive, subtle or otherwise, are administered to promote proper behavior.
- The Situation. Including adoption, foster care, school, summer camp, marriage, job, family, death.

I am proposing something in addition ... an occasional, temporary change of venue, a vacation, a Month in the Country, a visit to grandma's; a moment to let things settle, a retreat to find one's self and perhaps to think through next steps, a time moreover in a new context there to be viewed through the eyes of new people as well as a time to imagine anew and even to experiment with who one has been and now is and is becoming and would like to be.

The proposal I have in mind is situational and not at all dependent on expert input, authority, expertise or management but rather offers opportunity in the form of respite. Professionals ruin it by virtue of their professionalism just as in some religions including Voudun, the leader of the service must not be paid because that would remove him or her from the community.

It is the community, transitional in the case of the Clearing, not the skill of the professional nor the magic of the method that is the driving force. We refer here to something quite ordinary but which can be received as a considerable gift by the recipient.

Caveat: The short term venue will only be of use if it is infused with a welcoming presence seen in the art, architecture as well as in the person of the *Maître d'Hôte*, not a priest but rather a familiar figure whose manifestation might well be that of a fuddy-duddy in the eyes of the outsider but perhaps a grandpa or grandma figure to the child.

Adults hanging out in such a magic venue, a witch's house, a park, a school, an orphanage, a priut, find that playing a critical role in the life of the child is far from a simple thing.

When dealing with needy children, the question is how the roles of those who would help are presented and played out. In my view, a quiet, non-demanding, welcoming presence must underlie everything although depending on the individual this may be conveyed in various ways often mystifying to the observer, while the subtext is perfectly clear to the child.

Texts include the grouchy, the disinterested, the preoccupied and the demeaning. The subtext is acceptance, delight and a most gracious welcome.

"Ambience" is the watchword again.

Child Care

What Is Needed to Make It Possible for an Alienated, Unhappy Child to Become Part of Humanity While Glowing With Confidence and High Spirits? Normally, one discusses such matters through the medium of psychotherapeutic language which in this book I have tried to avoid.

I shall proceed to list those necessary conditions not in order of importance but rather as they come to mind.

1. A home base. This is usually taken to mean a roof, a bed, and food as well as family normally assumed to include a mother, a father and siblings. Sometimes uncles, aunts and grandparents. Plus a dog. There are, however, many possible variations on this arrangement from street gangs to orphanages.

2. An alternative base. This is located somewhere in the world and may include friends, a teacher, an institution such as a school or a club; uncles, aunts and grandparents—especially their homes.

3. For many people, the alternative base is religion in which the congregation is that against which the home base, the family of origin, is measured.

4. The sense of the self as the same as other selves and thus part of the public scene yet at once different, personal, indeed unique. Sameness is the prerequisite for affiliation with others, a recognition of that which is held in common. It may be expressed in the language of religion, nationality, tribe, team or organizational membership. However, if one acknowledges no more than group identity, he or she wanders in a gray morass. It is not enough to say, "I am of the Blue Team" because it references nothing beyond the parochial group and avoids the matter of who you may be uniquely; personally. It also offers no clues as to your relation to humanity at large. To qualify as fully human, one must come eventually to say, "I am me among all others" and to have a feel for what that implies.

5. A sense of time, of the history both of the period of one's own life and that of generations past. This intuition as projected toward the future provides a repository of goals, personal or communitarian; and for what one may or ought to strive for personally, socially or in the imagination.

6. An ethic of care versus one of contention. To blossom as an individual and to guarantee a full flowering of the community in which one is immersed, a sense of care for life itself must be held. It helps if one has been cared for adequately as a child but even if not, every child should have the experience of caring for another, a younger sibling, a parent, a friend; especially a dog.

7. Ownership of the mind. Through affirmation by others, teachers and parents as well as peers, the child's own perceptions of the world need to be affirmed and, through experience and conversation, elaborated and refined. This may be seen in the contribution of the arts to the lives of children.

8. Reflection. For a child to mature in our—or indeed any—society, time and means must be made available for reflection, for mulling things over, for finding one's way through the morass of opportunities and impediments that constitute life experience, for achieving wisdom even though that may not manifest itself until old age if then, too late to have practical import. In many cultures religious institutions play a key role in generating and supporting this kind of understanding. Our own society which is nominally secular, provides other vehicles. Chief among these are literature, theater, sports, art and music. By means of such routes, the developing child experiments with ways of relating to the larger world, arriving hopefully at ever more beguiling and effective solutions. Without reflection, one runs the risk of settling into uninspired compromises with reality, a routine existence ending in a default position consisting of action without foreseeing consequences whether pleasurable or unpleasant to the person, or of benefit or harm to the world at large.

9. Release. A child must eventually be released however gradually from the home into the fresh air, the common. This moment is a good one for rehearsing whatever he or

she wishes to become. We call the process "individuation" or better, "Education." Its vehicles include music, art, sport, industry, politics, science and enterprise.

Education is a process of liberation that constantly generates feedback. It ferments in the child's mind as a maturing sense of self. In so doing, a clearer vision of the world emerges and is tested. Understanding is transformed and elaborated upon ultimately to form the basis of yet further attempts to cope with Objective Reality, that complex union of provisional truth with all that is or might be.

Somewhere along the way one might consider that the child has found a god of sorts.

XIII

Haiti

It was the winter of 2005. I rode into town on the bed of a pickup truck that was loaded with American volunteers. The truck drove us from Lavale way up in the mountains where our program was held down to Jacmel, the beautiful Haitian coastal city.

As I descended the truck, a middle-aged fellow came up to me and said, "*I know you!* Where is your daughter?" His smile revealed several black holes that had once contained teeth.

He was peddling Cuban cigars. He displayed them in a tray that he held in front of him.

"But I am afraid I don't remember you," I said.

"Ah," he explained, "you and your daughter visited Jacmel in 1980. You hung around with us kids. They called me 'Ti Frère then, Little Brother. I was seven years old."

"Yes," I said vaguely, searching my memory. "I do remember. Of course. You look different now, 'Ti Frère."

Alice was twenty-one at the time. She had become interested in Haitian culture. With some anxiety mixed with a sense of adventure, I had accompanied her, "to protect her," I told myself.

We went to Jacmel then because we were told that it was a worthwhile tourist destination. But once there we discovered how sad a place it was. A few years prior to our visit, François—"Papa Doc"—Duvalier had carried out a massacre of Jacmel's mixed race population. That history combined with the near absence of electricity gave the town an ominous feel especially at night.

Alice had a great way with children. We were followed everywhere by street kids, mostly boys but some girls. We joked with them in our broken French—which, as Créole speakers, they could barely understand. They begged us for money but we gave them very little. They were poor and we felt sorry for them but we did not think that handing out money would do anybody much good. Mostly we just hung out.

During the course of our visit, Alice became ill with a high fever. 'Ti Frère happened upon us as we were wending our clueless way to our hotel through the black night after a visit to a doctor in his unsanitary office at the local hospital. We were, frankly, lost. Alice could barely walk.

"What is the matter with *Alice?*" 'Ti Frère asked. "Oh," I said. "She is very sick."

"*Wait!*" 'Ti Frère said. He disappeared. Moments later the street was swarming with boys two of whom encouraged Alice lean on them. Others carried our luggage. All together they led us to our hotel.

"Thank you," I said. Then I added, "You kids are always begging for money. I hardly ever gave you any. But this time you were very, very helpful and you deserve to get paid." With that, I handed out "Gourds," the Haitian currency.

But they handed the bills right back. "We didn't do this for *money,*" 'Ti Frère said. "We did this for *Alice.*"

That is the story 'Ti Frère recalled almost thirty years later.

Aftermath

It was October, 2011. I stepped off the battered bus in Lavale. We came from Port au Prince after a five hour, forty mile journey much of which was on the dusty mountain road that wound its way high above the fourteen settlements that constitute the township of La Vallée de Jacmel. La Vallée in Creole is written "Lavale." It is a valley only with respect to that particular road which runs above it. Lavale is in fact an area high on an heavenly mountain range when viewed from the seacoast city of Jacmel hundreds of meters below.

'Ti Ma's father met me at the bus stop. He embraced me as a dear friend and offered me a tangerine. "Welcome to Paradise," he said in Creole. "You must be tired from your long journey."

"No," I said, "I am all right. It is so very nice to be here."

"And to breathe the pure and pleasant air of Lavale. It is paradise here," he added. "Don't you agree?"

"Yes," I said. "I certainly do." After a momentary pause, I added awkwardly, "Lavale so different from Port-auPrince. Is there much crime here?"

"Our crime rate," he said, "has always been approximately zero."

Dreams

I dream of Haiti, odd, anxiety-driven reveries that reflect in precise detail that awe-full place, its fantasies flavored with both danger and attraction and both reluctance to remain and desire to return.

Last night I dreamed that I was in a Haitian mountain outhouse buzzing and crawling with huge insects. I could not manage to clean neither myself nor the floor around me. There was no indication that this was taking place in the Haiti of my mind but I knew that it was.

On another night I dreamed that I was walking along a beautiful, flower-lined street in what was certainly Haiti and I thought, "This place is as it always was. There are no problems."

I am returning to Haiti. Shortly. In two weeks I shall be there. I am eager to go. But I am also reluctant, more than reluctant. I imagine that I am on a high diving board or at the door of an airplane. I know I will jump but I am scared.

"Scared" is not the right word. It would be more accurate to say, "the prospect of visiting Haiti at this particular time concerns me." And why shouldn't it? On January 12th, 2010, Haiti was struck by a catastrophic earthquake. The country, already devoured by centuries of the most savage exploitation, was now reduced to rubble. Governments and agencies throughout the world have pledged assistance but little was delivered and much of what did arrive simply lined the pockets of corrupt schemers and officials and voracious foreign contractors all of whom were paid very well indeed.

I have not returned to Haiti since before that terrible event. I was simply chicken. I was also aware that the place was full of other white foreigners and that I had few if any unique skills to offer.

Another white guy without a clue.

Haiti has for years been a mecca for do-gooders and exploiters, some of them in one and the same person. There are more international Non-Governmental Organizations in Haiti than in any other country.

There are few if any tourists now but more chubby American missionaries and would-be go-gooders than in any place I know of or can imagine. But plenty of Peace Corps Volunteers, advisors, diplomats, hippies, drug dealers, child molesters, sex tourists, doctors, repatriated criminals, military brass, UN peace-keeping troops in blue helmets, contractors and consultants. This mix reached its frothy zenith right after the earthquake.

I am surely one of those do-gooders but did not choose to attend the feeding frenzy. I did not want to become yet another old white guy just hanging out, hands in pockets, with no relevant skills or money to offer. Worse, Haitians are deferent for the most part. I've stood on long line for a bus or one thing or another: "Let the old white guy go first," somebody would say and, to my utter humiliation, I would be shoved to the front.

Anyway, I didn't go to Haiti right after the earthquake. Was it because I did not want to be in the way or because I am a coward? A bit of each, I suppose. But now I am going.

Let us consider my goals for this forthcoming adventure. They are uncomplicated enough. I am curious. I want to see what's happening. I want to visit people and places that I have known and hear stories, particularly those having to do with how children and families have coped (or didn't cope) with the catastrophe.

I want to visit the people and projects with which I have worked over the years. I want to see what role they have played during the crisis and subsequent to it. Gody told me, for example, that two thousand children were evacuated from Port-au-Prince to Lavale, parentless and with little support. This in a town of four thousand people. How were they to be housed, fed, schooled? Gody said nevertheless that the local high school kids got together and organized assistance for these kids including a swiftly assembled elementary school run by the high schoolers. That is surely a story worth telling.

I want to speak with people in various organizations about the possibility of developing programs attractive to children, youth and communities and that might prove useful to them.

Finally, I want to speak with possible fiscal agents, particularly "Fonkoze," a progressive micro-finance bank, about becoming a single recipient of my contributions for various projects in Haiti, a co-planner with the community where each project is located, and the source of a monitoring and evaluation mechanism.

The goal is to simplify the raising of funds and getting me out of the position of having to deal with plethora of exotic groups while continuing to live in New England.

I anticipate that this will be my last visit to Haiti. It will be my nineteenth. I am, after all, getting old, terribly, sadly, creakily old. I will be eighty next summer. That puts me now in my eightieth year and the start of my ninth decade.

Too much. Way too much.

Recent History

From the "London Independent," September 19, 2010

"Today, I want to tell you the story of how our governments have been torturing and tormenting an island in the Caribbean - but it is a much bigger story than that. It's a parable explaining one of the main reasons how and why, across the world, the poor are kept poor, so the rich can be kept rich. If you grasp this situation, you will see some of the ugliest forces in the world laid out before you - so we can figure out how to stop them.

"The rubble-strewn island of Haiti is now in the middle of an election campaign that will climax this November. So far, the world has noticed it solely because the Haitian-American musician Wyclef Jean wanted to run for President, only to be blocked because he hasn't lived in the country since he was a kid. But there is a much bigger hole in the election: the most popular politician in Haiti by far, Jean-Bertrand Aristide. He's not there because, after winning a landslide election, he followed the will of the Haitian people who demanded he take on the multinational corporations and redistribute enough money that their children wouldn't starve - so our governments had him kidnapped him at gunpoint and refuse to let him back.

"But we have to start a little earlier if this is going to make sense. For over two centuries, Haiti has been effectively controlled from outside. The French enslaved the entire island in the eighteenth century and worked much of the population to death, turning it into the sugar and coffee plantation for the world.

By this century, Western governments were arming, funding and fueling the psychopathic dictatorship of the Duvalier family - who slaughtered 50,000 people - supposedly because they were "our friends" in the fight against communism.

"All this left Haiti the most unequal country in the world. A tiny elite lives in vast villas in the hills, while below and all around them, the overwhelming majority of the population live in tiny tin shacks with no water or electricity, crammed six-to-a-room. Just 1 per cent own 50 per cent of the wealth and 75 per cent of the arable land. Once the Haitian people were finally able to rise up in 1986 to demand democracy, they obviously wanted the country's wealth to be shared more fairly. They began to organize into a political movement called Lavalas - the flood - to demand higher wages and higher taxes on the rich to build schools and hospitals and subsidies for the half-starved poor. This panicked the elite.

"And nobody panicked them more than a thin, softly-spoken, intellectual slum-priest named Aristide who found himself at the crest of this wave. He was born into a bitingly poor family and became a brilliant student. As a priest he soon became one of the leading exponents of Liberation Theology, the left-wing Catholicism that says that people shouldn't wait passively for justice in the Kingdom of Heaven, but must demand it here and now. Aristide explained: "The rich of my country, a tiny percentage, sit at a vast table overflowing with good food, while the rest of my countrymen are crowded under that table, hunched in the dirt and starving. One day the people under the table will rise up in righteousness."

"On this platform, he was elected in 1990 in a landslide in the country's first free and fair election, taking 64 per cent of the vote. He kept his promise to the Haitian people: he increased the minimum wage from 38 cents a day to $1, demanding the multinational corporations pay a less insulting wage. He trebled the number of free secondary schools. He disbanded the murderous national army that had terrorized the population. Even the International Monetary Fund had to admit that over the Aristide period and just after, Haiti's Human Poverty Indicator - a measure of how likely your kids are to die, starve or go uneducated - dropped dramatically from 46.2 per cent to 31.8 per cent.

"But why would foreign governments care about a small country, the poorest in the Western hemisphere, with only ten million inhabitants? Ira Kurzban, an American lawyer based in Haiti, explains: "Aristide represented a threat to [foreign powers] because he spoke for the 85 per cent of his population who had never been heard. If that can happen in Haiti, it can happen anywhere, including in countries where the [US and Europe] have huge economic interests and extract natural resources. They don't want real popular democracies to spread because they know it will confront US economic interests." Oxfam called this phenomenon "the threat of a good example."

"So after Haiti had experienced seven months of democracy, the US toppled Aristide. Ordinary Haitians surrounded his home, calling for his return - and they were fired on so indiscriminately that more ammo had to be sent from Guantanamo Bay on Cuba. Their bodies were left in the streets to be eaten by dogs as the advances were repealed one by one.

"In 1994, the Clinton administration agreed to return Aristide to power - provided he castrate his own political program and ignore the demands of his people. They made him agree to privatize almost everything, freeze wages, and sack half the civil service. Through gritted teeth, he agreed, and for the remainder of his time in office tried to smuggle through what little progress he could. He was re-elected in an even bigger landslide in 2000 - but even his tiny shuffles towards redistribution were too much. The US and French governments had Aristide kidnapped at gunpoint and dumped him in the Central African Republic. They said he was a "dictator", even though the last Gallup poll in a free Haiti found 60 per cent supported him, compared to just 3 per cent backing the alternative imposed on the country by the US.

"The human rights situation in Haiti then dramatically deteriorated, with a massive campaign of terror and repression. The Lavalas Party was banned from running again, with most of the country's democracy activists jailed. There were huge military assaults on the slums which demanded Aristide's return. A US Army Psychological Operations official explained the mission was to ensure Haitians "don't get the idea they can do whatever they want."

"The next President, Rene Préval, learned his lesson: he has done everything he was told to by corporations and governments, privatizing the last remaining scraps owned by the state, and using tear gas to break up strikes for higher wages. The Haitian people rejected the whole rigged electoral process, with turn-out falling to just 11 per cent. Today, Aristide is a broken man, living in exile in South

Africa, studying for a Ph.D. in linguistics, banned from going home.

"This is part of a pattern. When poor countries get uppity and tried to ask for basic justice, our governments have toppled them, from Iran wanting to control its own oil in 1953 to Honduras wanting its workers to be treated decently in 2009. You don't have to overthrow many to terrify the rest.

"It doesn't have to be this way. This is not the will of the people in the US or Europe. On the contrary, ordinary citizens are horrified "when the propaganda is stripped away and they see the truth. It only happens because a tiny wealthy elite dominates our foreign policy and uses it to serve their purposes – low wages and control of other people's economies and resources. The people of Haiti, who have nothing, were bold and brave enough to campaign and organize to take power back from their dreadful elite classes.

"Are we?"

XIV

Journaling

I am returning to Haiti again—for the 19th time—in just two weeks, my first visit since the earthquake. My goal is to become a journalist, to report back to the US what I see; and it is simply to learn. A subsidiary goal is to consult with a few educational and social community-based projects, each initiated by Haitians, and to find ways to support them. I have been doing that sort of thing for some time.

The article above? Good as general background. But as you can imagine, I do not consider Aristide a likely savior of his country. While I do not believe that the US had a right to depose him, he was by the time he left, deeply compromised by corruption, privatization of key industries, and generally presented a less than progressive or reliable face to the people. He was hewing to a Neo-liberal line already on his return from refuge in the US. The guys in Washington got to him. But he proved not to be a reliable ally.

They never trusted him anyway. They considered him a dangerous kook. He had trouble with Haitians as well. By the time of his departure he had lost the support of much of the left although he did certainly retain the admiration of the majority of the peasantry.

Rene Préval, his chosen successor, was not bad but he was weak, bland, the opposite end of the charisma continuum from Aristide.

The politics of that country seem always to have been at once weird and atrocious as have been the relations between Haiti and the US. Fortunately, my interest is not in politics. I avoid discussions of politics—as well as religion—when I am there. My focus is on educational, community-based programs for children.

September 30, 2010 Thursday

It must be stated re: my interest in this sad country that, though historically more isolated from the world than most, it is also an iconic case study of relations between Great Powers and poor, easily exploitable people, in Haiti's case: slaves, and those who own something that the big guys believe that they must have, including sugar, strategic location, and more recently, bauxite from which aluminum is produced.

Next item of importance: I broke my upper left canine tooth the other day. Consultation with both a general dentist and a periodontist suggested that it will be a big deal to repair, necessitating a hard yank, root canal work, bone grafting and an implant. The cost will be in the neighborhood of five thousand dollars of which as much as half could be covered by insurance. I decided to get a second opinion from my former periodontist in Burlington, Vermont, but, since I am off to Haiti in less than a week, this won't take place until I return. The local dentist stabilized the wagging, broken tooth with cement. But that was two days ago and it is coming loose again.

(Is it possible to go to Haiti in such a condition? Wouldn't I be well advised to remain home and take care of my teeth?)

I try not to worry about the Haitians who survive in fragile tents blown away by autumn storms while suffering wounds, fractures, hunger, exposure to the elements, loss and untold psychic trauma.

October 4, 2010

On the train from Washington, DC. where we attended a memorial for a friend:

Haiti still is far away although tomorrow at this time I will be preparing for landing at the Maîs Gaté Airport. What a funny name, *Maîs Gaté*! It means "Rotten Corn" in French. How apt.

It is raining heavily as the train lobs along the Northeast Corridor. We were in Washington to mourn a friend who died recently. Does the rain reflect sadness? For the friend? For the Haitian millions who lost their loved ones and homes in the recent catastrophe? Or is it of no significance at all, god being busy watching fallen sparrows?

Ives,[9] my Haitian friend, long time hustler once on the streets of New York, now Port-au-Prince; at least partially reformed addict who is sharp, knowledgeable, able to get you anything you want, a man who speaks Creole like a Haitian and English like a New Yorker, one of the best Haitian Virgils who has ushered me through the various levels of Haiti's hell. Ives, who offered to bring together twelve ("Ives," I begged, "no more than FOUR!") people of the streets and the parks to be interviewed about what, I do not remember, probably their lives and their boundless trauma.

The plan today is again to collect stories so that I may retell them back home. The most useful role for me here is probably that of story-collector. Photographer, too. It is to bring about a glimmer of visibility to this unseen and perhaps unseeable country.

I will meet the interviewees Ives collects later today at La Terrace Cafe, a charming place up high in Petionville. It is owned and operated by an American husband and wife team who have lived in Haiti for many years. Along the way they have quietly helped countless Haitians of the streets including Holner La Tendresse, the recently deceased Grand Dame of the *Sans Manmans* ("without mothers," i.e. vagabonds) who was often fed there for free.

The people will come, Ives warned me, but mostly for food. I don't mind, I said. I will gladly treat them as long as they consent to honest interviews. But, thought I, journalists worth their salt never pay for such. Will my free meals compromise credibility?

---

[9] Not his real name

October 6, 2010

The plane landed yesterday. From the window I noted the greenery beyond the runway. The small houses beyond were whitewashed and probably pretty. The blue and white plastic of the tents now just beneath us provide temporary shelter for the displaced.

The airport buildings did not appear damaged. In fact, a major expansion of the airport seemed to be in progress. We debarked along one of those long, portable, enclosed corridors common in major airports everywhere in the world. Retrieving baggage was a frustrating hassle but no worse than at JFK, Logan, or LA.

Carla met me in a four wheeler along with three other passengers. Carla and her husband, Ron, white Americans, have been living in Haiti for about thirty years. They and their Haitian friends have created an organization, "*N a Sonje*," We Will Remember." It presents Haitian history in song and theater.

In frequent consultation with journalists and diplomats, Carla and Ron are entirely admirable people. We drove to their home compound up high in the mountains beyond Petionville in the scraggly town of *Gwo Jan*, "Big John."

The destruction caused by the earthquake barely reached there. Haiti itself generally seemed to be pretty much as I had known it for these many years. Thirty or so. Remarkable ... but, as I was soon to learn, my impression was only partially valid.

I was very tired, not having slept much the night before. I had caught the Super Shuttle bus from Manhattan to JFK at four-thirty A.M. And here I was with Carla in Gwo Jan talking and talking into what seemed dawn but was actually only seven-thirty PM at which point I collapsed onto her guest bed and did not gain consciousness until six-thirty AM or thereabouts and talked some more. We yammered away some more and yet again more. The conversation was largely about Haitian culture and history as reflected in the character of various individuals we knew and their roles in social organization.

At lunch time Carla drove me to La Terrace Cafe in Petionville where I met with Ives, the quick-witted, friend born in Haiti, raised a New Yorker; speaks with an undiminished New York accent; hustler, man of the streets, former addict and confirmed manipulator but neither a fully dishonest nor actual criminal sort.

I once paid to for Ives to undergo drug treatment in a Haitian program, not a very good one as it turned out, but in my encounters with him over the past several years he has seemed clean. He claims to want to help people and has indeed been useful in guiding tourists, reporters and diplomats around Port au Prince. Ives can have an almost pleasant, ingratiating manner but can also come across as imperious.

I ran by my program ideas with both Carla and Ives. They both liked them and provided me with helpful feedback.

Thursday, October 7, 2010

Six twenty-six in the morning. I hear the rush of the water in the brook only a few yards from the house. Everyone is asleep. I woke up an hour ago. The air is warm but not oppressively so. It rained last night as it has done each night for weeks they tell me. Neither bugs, flies, nor mosquitoes announce themselves. There are no screens on the windows and doors in Carla's house. That seemed odd at first.

We are high in the mountains above Port-au-Prince and just beyond Petionville. It is not very far from here to the center of the city. We are in something like a suburb. But it feels remote. One needs to travel a long, scarcely maintained dirt road to get here. Carla explained that in a country where almost no one owns a vehicle, there is little motivation to keep a road in good shape.

A cock crows. A dog barks. Otherwise, silence.

Yesterday, after lunch and conversation, Ives accompanied me on a stroll around town. We went through the large camp where hundreds of refugees from January's earthquake are living in extremely close proximity to one another in Petionville's elite town center. The encampment is directly opposite the city hall, near the famous church, and across the street from the elegant Kinam Hotel which is still standing and still host to NGO officials, military brass, missionaries and myriad consultants. There are no tourists in Haiti.

The scene seemed surprisingly normal and had the feel of permanence. Children played, women scrubbed their laundry in tubs and then hung out to dry on jerry-rigged lines; sidewalk vendors displayed their wares of fruits, vegetables, miscellaneous hardware and old clothes. A temporary bandstand was set up in the center of the camp. Music groups, Ives explained, often visit. Except for one guy who aggressively demanded ten dollars from me, no beggars approached nor did I seem the object of curiosity. There were no police in evidence although I noticed a temporary, wooden structure with a sign on it indicating that it was the "Ministry for the Protection of Haitian Women."

It was indeed an Haitian village, more crowded than most but indistinguishable from many. Except for the fact that people lived in tents rather than houses and that many of these were frayed or torn and were set on ground that turned to mud in the rain that came cascading down regularly every evening, it was an ordinary town, normal and likely to remain in place for a long time.

Ives was amazed, he said, that the camp had not been devastated by disease; cholera had just begun to reach Port au Prince.

Unfortunately, Ives never found anybody for me to interview.

Carla and I talked last evening and this morning about what she calls the "crabs in a barrel" phenomenon. It is said that if you put a bunch of crabs in a barrel and one of them tries to escape by climbing up the side, the others will pull him back down. That, Carla said, is the paradigm for what happens when an individual Haitian attempts to pull him or her away from the community in favor of individual advancement. The community will yank that person right back down again.

At the same time, I imagine, this would make the role of the community leader, the *Gwo Neg*, the big man, that much more attractive, conferring on such a person considerable power over the others. He is the puller rather than the pulled.

It might also represent roots of inertia on the one hand and corruption on the other. If there is no power to transcend the community, those who nevertheless succeed in doing so become the very embodiment of the power of that community.

Much that we see in the Haitian character may be traced to the history of slavery. There is surprising calm on the one hand and a strong communitarian ethos on the other with a substrate under both of jealousy and an obsessive scratching for position and personal survival. Periodically there is a predictable explosion.

Amateur social science perhaps yet perhaps with a grain of truth.

Once not so long ago I ran into an American soldier in the airport waiting room. He was an officer responsible, among other things, for keeping statistics on violent crime in Haiti. "What is remarkable," he said, "is how little there is in Haiti, such a poor country and with such a terrible history. We have much more violence in any of our major US cities."

October 7, 2010

Now I am in a guest house in the Delmas neighborhood of downtown Port-au-Prince. I signed out of Carla's house and N a Sonje in Gwo Jan. I want to be near the humane girls' orphanage with which I am still somewhat involved, "*Le Foyer des Filles de Dieu*," (the Hearth of the Girls of God). It was founded and continues to be run by the indomitable Mme Paula Thybulle, "*Mulatto*," a condition that translates as "upper class and disinterested in the great sea of poverty in which one is immersed." But Paula, despite what are conservative politics, does not fit the stenotype. She has devoted her life to the children under her care and, although stern when needed, she has a famous heart of gold. The girls call her "*Manman Paula.*"

Paula is a naturalized US citizen and has lived for some twenty-five years in the New York area. She was trained there in social work. She then returned to Haiti to serve abandoned and abused children. Mme Paula is a saint in the minds of many.

The *pension* in which I now reside is a ten minute walk to Mme Paula's orphanage. My thought was to visit it tomorrow. And I will. But just a little while ago I called her to let her know my plans. In a weak voice she told me that she is in hospital. She was brought there today. I spoke with her friend and physician, Dr. LaPLanche, director of the community health clinic affiliated with the orphanage. Dr. LaPlanche said that Paula is probably suffering from pneumonia.

I am concerned. I am concerned for Paula but even more for her girls. I cannot imagine what will happen to them if Paula becomes unable to function.

The next morning

I visited the orphanage first thing to see how everybody is doing. The residence had been seriously damaged by the earthquake. Almost all the kids were in the yard by the gate at the time of the collapse so fortunately no one was in the building when it collapsed. Three girls, however, were visiting the school's cook at her home which collapsed totally. All three girls, the cook and her family were killed.

I was welcomed most warmly with songs, hugs and giggles.

I will talk with Dr. LaPlanche later and somehow get to the hospital to see Paula. My plan after that is to head to Leogane, the small city that was at the epicenter of the earthquake. It will be a long day.

But plans changed. Carla showed up at Le Foyer and drove me to the offices of Fonkoze, an exemplary national micro-lending "people's" bank. There I conferred with Ann Hastings, the executive director. I asked if it might be possible for Fonkoze to become my fiscal agent for the various groups with which I work, distributing contributions not only from me but from other concerned Americans and then doing the necessary "due diligence" follow-up.

I left Ann's office convinced that such a plan was a good one.

Charitable giving is tricky. Mary and I are hardly rich by US standards but even our modest contributions seem like a lot in a poor country; they have considerable power both to help and to corrupt.

We can only function as do-gooders by working through an organization that we can trust.

Since in Haiti there is no government worth talking about at this time, we must work through the best Non-Governmental Organization we can find, one that seems to have its nose to the ground.

Carla then drove me through the tangled mass of traffic in downtown Port-au-Prince. We did not happen to pass the government and financial center that has reportedly been utterly destroyed, "a message from God," it is said. But we did go down Avenue Grand Delmas and through some of side streets I had known. We also visited two friends of Carla's who live as organizers in a tent encampment.

Destruction was everywhere, some dramatic as in the case of the utter elimination of The Caribbean Market, a large, popular center, where many shoppers and clerks were killed. Some buildings did remain untouched. But what stood out for me was the steady drumbeat ... a collapsed house here and another there, rocks, chips of cement and trash, all left as they were, uncollected; ignored.

Yet throngs of people continued about their daily business, chatting, running, strolling, carrying loads in their hands or on their heads. Through disaster, I sensed the incongruous presence of the workaday world.

Carla and I bade each other a fond farewell. She is a fine hostess and she and Ron, her husband, have for a great many years done impressive community work in this country. They are white American ex-patriots with no thought of ever returning to the

States. Despite everything, they believe that interpersonally Haiti is a healthier and happier place to live than is the US.

Ann Hastings, the key Fonkoze person with whom I met, is also a white American who has lived here for many years. She has the same perspective. Her work brings her often to the States. But once there, having finished her work and visiting her grandchildren, she cannot wait to get back to her home in Haiti.

Haiti is a beautiful country now experiencing one of the worst times in its ghastly history and yet ... and yet ... and yet there is something strangely attractive about the place even now. It casts a Voudon spell.

Wall's Guest House overflows with missionaries. I don't know how many, certainly well over a dozen. They don't seem particularly intrusive in the sense of pushing their particular god, an enterprise common enough in this country with so many gods. Another one or two here or there would do no harm. But what strikes me is that these ecclesiastic Americans are just so, how can I put it? ... classically American. They tend to be overweight for the most part, wear short pants, drink beer and talk and laugh loudly all of that with an assumed but unmerited and rather unattractive authority.

On the other hand, the goal of those at the table to my right is to build houses for the homeless, not a bad idea on the face of it.

But who told them that Haitians require American labor? Haitians are famously good workers and chronically unemployed. In the second place, how do they know that the design of their constructions will meet Haitian requirements? I mean, how well do they know the country, the customs, and the local people? About as well as we know Afghanis and Iraqis, I suspect.

In that next table the four of them are loudly discussing how they will go about the building project. One fellow seems to be well informed on technical matters so he is holding forth. The other three are not bad on that sort of stuff either.

What the central guy is proposing is a house with a tin roof. I had earlier asked him if a tin roof would not transmit fierce, tropical heat to the people under it. Might not insulation of some sort help, I asked? He explained that tin reflects the sun's rays and that the roof would be so constructed as to leave a gap between the two halves such that hot air would flow right out. "It is easily ten degrees cooler on the inside under these conditions than on the outside," he said. He added that his houses will also be earthquake and hurricane resistant. His intention is to instruct Haitians on his design.

But what I did not ask him—I was tired again and ready for a nap—is "Why not consult an actual Haitian?" Although in Port-au-Prince and other cities, people have been building concrete houses with cement roofs because they seem to guarantee solidity and permanence, in the hustings, however, thatched roof, pole-frame buildings have been in style for centuries, millennia if you include Africa. These buildings are practical in that they remain cool inside, can be constructed according to local design, are made of local materials by local labor, and hurricanes or earthquakes or may easily be rebuilt.

A key advantage is that they are made entirely by materials readily available locally.

Americans famously tend to march right in with a packaged solution the result of which are costs beyond the means of ordinary people and require that funds are spent on products manufactured and sold in the United States.

The Russian word, "*samadour,*" is applicable here. It refers to someone with a take-charge attitude who doesn't know what he (or she) is talking about.

Along with American missionaries, a dozen or so Haitians live here as well, maybe temporarily, maybe as transients. Some or all work as cooks, guards and cleaning women. My room is in the midst of their quarters. It seems to be a multiple family scene. One family has two little children, girls, about three and one. And cute, cheerful, well behaved children they are.

It is good to live among the locals at a comfortable distance from my compatriots.

Le Foyer des Filles de Dieu

I had talked with Paula Thybulle on the phone this morning before leaving for Leogane and later with her friend and physician, Dr, LaPlanche in person. Paula is doing better and should be okay soon. I did not visit her because what with the traffic and the rubble, it would have taken the whole day. Instead, I visited her orphanage, Le Foyer des Filles de Dieu, The girls were delighted to see me. Right off the bat they wanted to know if I was going to take them to the beach—I had done so on my previous three or four visits. I answered that it depended on Mme Paula and the needs of the orphanage.

I hung around waiting for Dr. LaPlanche. She is the co-director of Le Foyer with Mme Thybulle and is primarily responsible for the affiliated community health clinic but she takes an active interest in the functioning of the entire operation. Dr. LaPlanche is an attractive, stylishly dressed, middle aged woman. She is light-skinned, educated in France and has more the manner of an upper class European than a Haitian. She is gracious and businesslike rather than actually warm.

While hanging out, I spent most of my time sitting in the courtyard with children all around me, touching my skin, sitting on my lap, asking questions, looking at pictures on my iPod, taking a few more shots with my camera, but most of all simply being very close to me as well as to one another.

One girl introduced her sisters, one ten and the other seven. She herself is eleven.

"How long have you been here?" I asked.

"Two years," she said.

"And why are you here?"

"Our mother died of the fever. And our father has no work. He cannot take care of us."

"It is sad to lose a mother," I ventured. "You must miss her."

"We do."

"Do you take care of each other."

"We do."

"Do you like it here?"

"We do."

I soon met with Dr. LaPlanche who was worried about the financial state of the orphanage. Paula is responsible for seventy-two children but has barely enough money to feed them. She could not send them to school this week for lack of funds and is concerned about next week when the prospect of getting them back into school again seems remote.

Dr. LaPlanche believes that Paula's illness was precipitated by the extreme financial stress that she has been under.

I explained that when I take the children to the beach it costs me about three hundred dollars. Perhaps, I suggested, it would be more helpful if I were simply to hand that money to the orphanage so that the children can go to school next week. Dr. LaPlanche immediately agreed. She assigned a young man, a staff member, to accompany me back to the hotel where I wrote out a check for five hundred dollars which he then brought to Dr. LaPlanche.

Just prior to leaving, I said to a group of girls, "Unfortunately, the orphanage needs my money for you to go to school next week. Sadly, it is more important that you go to school than that you go to the beach. I am so sorry."

They stared at me silently. A few nodded their heads. I don't think they were convinced. Dr. LaPlanche promised to discuss this with them later.

The guy in charge of Wall's Guest House in Port-au-Prince found someone who was willing to transport me to Leogane at a fair price—$100 US. The driver, Bruce, brought his friend, John, along with him. Both are good guys. John speaks some English and fair French which, he said, he learned on his own. Bruce speaks only Creole.

It took several hours to navigate the thirty or so miles from Port-au-Prince to Leogane. The roads were in dreadful condition replete with pot holes and crevices. For much of the trip a fog of dust and sand particles hung over everything. Traffic jams were almost continuous. Neighborhoods I had known were totally destroyed— Belleville, Bizoton, Carrefour, Mariani.

The two drivers asked me for the address of the guest house. "62, rue La Croix," I told them, forgetting that because of the earthquake the house had been destroyed and that the entire operation had moved to the countryside. It was now in "Mon Petit Village," a mile or two from the city.

It was then that we became aware of the astounding destruction of Leogane. I plan to walk through it again tomorrow in order to photograph the scene and to talk with anyone I meet.

October 8, 2010

… And now I am in Leogane. The earthquake rendered this town unimaginably devastated. The Haitian guys who drove me here were astounded … and they live in Port au Prince which was not spared. But Leogane is many times worse. On Rue La Croix where the Gateau Guest House once stood and where its empty shell remains, almost every house is gone, utterly disappeared. Flattened. A pile of broken cement walls, pebbles and sand. I knew the street well but could not determine exactly where I now stood. A nightmare.

How many human bodies remain under that rubble?

I have moved on to Mon Petit Village. Where I sit at the moment it is quite the opposite of what we saw in the city. It is beautiful … even though tents for displaced families surround us.

Yoleine Gateau-Esposito is co-director of Mon Petit Village— and co-founder with James Philemy—of "the NEGES Foundation," its parent organization, an indigenous Haitian NGO. Both Yoleine and James are Haitian-Americans who live in Brooklyn. They work as educators there yet manage to be in Leogane as often as once a month where they create and lead a conglomeration of most impressive programs.

Thanks to the destruction of their entire Leogane operation, they have moved everything out a couple of miles to the countryside, to "Mon Petit Village," a stretch of land with small buildings surrounded by pastures. This is where I am now typing and where we held a work camp five years ago the purpose of which was to transform old automobile tires into planters for trees and flowering bushes.

At the moment Mon Petit Village is full with people, tents and a central laundry facility. In the sheltered "kiosk," where we had gathered for celebrations and meetings when I was last here with the volunteers, now children—most of them boys; one, a girl—dressed in white uniforms are practicing karate moves. They run, jump, kick and punch, a graceful, disciplined, dance-like sport.

I am with a half-dozen young men. We are sitting on the porch of the main house where we are discussing the miracle of modern technology, the iPod Touch especially if used in concert with the very cool Bluetooth keyboard that I use. Many young men in Haiti, notably John and another guy whose name I didn't catch, are well informed on matters of technology. It is remarkable that in such a low tech country we find a proliferation of technologically sophisticated youth.

One of the guys, Edy, has an iPhone of his own given him by an American volunteer but it is damaged and barely works. We considered the advantages and disadvantages of network-based telephone systems such as Skype versus those with cell phone company contracts.

8:28 AM

I slept well enough. The shower at Mon Petit Village is excellent even though it offered only cold water. But in these tropical climes, cold water is actually way warmer than one would expect.

Molly is a young American in Haiti on her own. Last night, she and I talked with Jocelyn, a Haitian woman, best friend—"we are like sisters"—to Yoleine Gateau-Esposito, co-director of the NEGES Foundation. Jocelyn is in charge of the program in Yoleine's absence. Yoleine at the moment is in Brooklyn at her job as guidance director. But she returns to Haiti often. Her mother, who died last year at the age of ninety-six—just before the earthquake—was perhaps Leogane's most distinguished citizen. She was a strong woman, a Voudon priestess—a Mambo—honest, gracious and civic minded.

Jocelyn, a Haitian-born woman who has lived in the US for many years, has always longed to return to Haiti. "I love it here," she said. "I am not one who buys into the American Dream." Jocelyn, like Yoleine's mother, is a Mambo, a designation that suggests power derived from the spirits.

We talked about these matters late into the night—actually it was only about eight-thirty when I hit the sack but it felt much later.

Morning

Considering the earthquake, everything is surprisingly delightful and well functioning in Mon Petit Village this morning. The sun shines. Roosters crow and dogs bark.

The Karate boys—I see no girls—are up early, in uniform and once again busy practicing. They are quick and fierce and accompany each move with impressive grunts and shouts. The women have prepared a simple but hearty breakfast for us and are sweeping the yard. One old lady is doing my laundry unasked. I would have done it myself but it is better to pay her.

Yoleine had asked me to take some pictures. I am off to my photographic assignment.

October 9, 2010 ....

The "Photographic Assignment" turned out to be rather different than what I anticipated. Ricardo, one of the guys who hangs around here, an earnest, pleasant fellow, asked Molly and me if we would like to visit an orphanage just down the road. He used to work there, he explained, and added something to the effect that he himself had been raised in an orphanage although not that particular one. We were curious and agreed but I added a caveat that I was not about to hand out money to the orphanage today nor was I in a position to adopt anybody.

Agreed. Ricardo hailed two motorcycle taxis. He and Molly hopped on one and I mounted the other. Off we went about five miles down the road to "Lamb Missionary Orphanage" where we spent the better part of the morning.

Like most orphanages in Haiti, it is run by a fringe Protestant church. The Pastor introduced himself but his name didn't stick in my mind and I neglected to jot it down. I tend to be allergic to pastors but this one didn't seem so bad. There was something reasonable about the fellow. He did not attempt to press his religion on me and came across as primarily concerned with the welfare of the children. But who is to say? Orphanages are a very big business in Haiti as they are in much of the world.

The children stood by, watching us with sad eyes and endearing faces. There are thirty-six of them in his care between the ages of, I would judge, three and fourteen. There is a staff of nineteen, and no permanent building. Everyone lives in tents donated by UNICEF and USAID. The Pastor, cleanly dressed, competent appearing, explained that they do not have enough money to run the place properly. He showed me where the pump house had been. The earthquake destroyed it utterly.

"To get water, we send the children on a hike down the road to UNICEF headquarters with plastic milk jugs," he said. "It is impossible to take proper baths here or to wash clothes and the children barely have enough to drink. We don't have enough money to feed them properly or to pay our staff adequate salaries. Unfortunately, we are not affiliated with a partner church in the United States. We get a little help from UNICEF but it is not enough."

He never directly asked me for money.

We played with the children. I took many pictures and then the staff gathered everyone in the yard and got us all to sing songs together and play-party games.

It was sad to leave them. Molly said that she would volunteer to teach there one or two days a week.

We then went not far from the orphanage to see Lorene's baby and her one room rented from a local family. Lorene is a young woman who was raised in another orphanage, a cold, dreary place that I visited some years ago. When she reached age eighteen she was unceremoniously thrown out because the orphanage needed her bed. Yoleine, a tough woman with a famously soft heart, took her in and employed her at NEGES.

But Lorene had no relevant skills at all, not even of the simplest sort. She was emotionally needy and extremely vulnerable having had no experience in the world beyond the institutional walls. Sure enough, she quickly became pregnant by a guy she hardly knew. An American woman, a friend of mine, a Vermonter named Andrea, took pity on her during a visit. Andrea sent her gifts, funded her through a complicated pregnancy and even now pays for the rent of the room where she and her baby, seven months old and apparently healthy, live. Lorene named the baby "Andre" in honor of Andrea. Andrea refers to Lorene as "my daughter."

We returned to "Mon Petit Village" by tap-tap to Leogane followed by a motorcycle ride. I spent the afternoon on a hike to town to photograph the destruction caused by the earthquake which was extensive and infinitely sad. I had several brief encounters along the way with people—children most memorably—who wanted to know who I was and why I was there. I bought a funky straw hat from a street peddler. A straw hat is essential in a country where the sun seems to blaze inches above one's head.

While in Mon Petit Village, I was told that Molly had taken off down the busy highway on a bicycle that some of the young guys here had put together for her. That was some hours ago. Interesting news but not yet worrisome. It was only four in the afternoon.

But by six Molly had still not returned and it was getting dark. Jocelyn dispatched Markendy, a brilliant but marginally educated young man from a poor village, to go to town on his motorcycle, find her and bring her back. He returned an hour later. Unsuccessful.

★★★★

It is morning now. Seems that Molly returned after I was asleep. Americans are an odd lot, obsessed with security to the extent that we kill for it, nevertheless we go through life oblivious to blatant danger, believing in our soul that we are immortal. Haitians by contrast live with death, respect its inevitability and develop skills to handle daily contingencies and engage in a respectful dialogue with its omnipresence.

October 10, 2010

Molly woke up early, hopped on her bike and headed off but this time told Jocelyn where she was going and when she would return. I walked to Leogane myself somewhat later in order to change money. Even though it is Sunday, Pharmacie St. Michel is open and, according to Jocelyn, offers the best exchange rate.

On the way I ambled along taking more pictures even though I have more than enough already. When people asked, I told them that I am a journalist which is close to the truth.

As I began my hike back, Molly rode up, bright and cheery. We had a cool drink together at a stand that consisted of one small plastic cooler. Treat was on Molly. She told me that she and Jocelyn discussed her last night's behavior and she now realizes that she was in error not to have told anybody about when she intended to return. I added that the concern we all felt was partially for her well being but it was also organizational. If there are accidents or problems with people who volunteer with NEGES, its reputation becomes damaged locally and internationally. A good reputation is critical for support, both financial and within the local community.

Molly seems to have understood but she remains a very independent sort who believes that she can handle anything. She will probably be okay in the long run. It is the short run that Jocelyn and I worry about.

The afternoon: I am wandering alone around Leogane again, feeling perfectly safe, taking pictures, having brief interchanges with random people, sitting on a wall, watching the passing scene ... so many people living in tents, white ones presumably to reflect the heat which is formidable in Leogane, far more so than in Petionville where I was the other day or in Lavale where I will be on Tuesday. Both have the advantages of being on mountains. Leogane is at sea level.

I find it hard to do very much before I need to stop, drink water, take a nap and, if I am lucky, a shower. It is a slow, useless existence. Most Haitians seem to walk slowly here, often carrying things on their heads—buckets of water for the most part—women especially. But both sexes work very hard. I stood watching while a work crew of bare-shirted men formed a human chain to haul water buckets up a long ladder to the roof of a building that was being reconstructed. The water was needed for mixing concrete. The buckets were heavy but the men kept right on hauling, rapidly, bucket after bucket, for the longest time, sweat pouring from their naked backs; singing, shouting together, even cheerfully and without rest; a team, *"konbit"* in Creole.

People here live in occasional undamaged houses but many more have settled in tents, some manufactured and contributed by NGOs such as UNICEF and USAID but many dwellings are ramshackle sheds slapped together arbitrarily. While some people have knocked scraps of wood together to form some protection from the sun, others have displayed remarkable carpentry skills and have created tiny but actual houses for themselves and their families.

The other day when I was without my camera I saw people sitting under two upended mattresses that leaned against each other leaving a triangular living space underneath. It was gone today when I returned to record it.

There are many not so obvious problems. One was pointed out to me by the two guys who drove me here. It is this: Prior to the earthquake, most people had been paying rent for their living space. But in their current dwelling, hot, wet, minimal, vermin-ridden and uncomfortable though it may be, they pay nothing. *Gratis.* Furthermore, they are often provided free electricity—or they steal it—and are recipients besides of food and supplies thanks to generous international organizations and foreigners of good will. Thus, it is claimed, many people do not wish to be rehabilitated. They want to stay right where they are. Meanwhile, the government is so weak as to be virtually nonexistent. There is no one to persuade or require the disposed to live otherwise—and pay rent.

Today is Sunday. Not much going on. This evening, though, there is to be a Voudon demonstration event. Jocelyn, among other things, is a Voudon priestess, a *"Mambo."* Should be interesting.

October 11, 2010

I have a few moments to relax so I shall record a memorable episode.

But first: David. Molly found this guy, David, a Canadian computer geek and amateur economist, an odd, goose-necked fellow who goes to places like Haiti on his own where he attempts to practice his version of good works. Molly finds him interesting. So do I. David is highly critical of the work that NGOs do and wonders if any of them accomplish anything at all beyond raising money which then goes to purchase American-made products or simply to line the pockets of plutocrats, mostly the American ones. His critique is similar to my own but he is better informed and considerably crankier.

Take the matter of the tents. People steal these, David explained, and sell them at odious prices to others even though they were obtained for nothing. Whatever is donated becomes fuel for corruption. And the NGOs, with their heads in the clouds and noses far from the ground, have no idea what is going on and seem to care less thus further opening the door to anarchy.

David's solution for post-catastrophe intervention whether in Haiti or elsewhere is simply to hand people money *gratis* to enable them to purchase locally whatever they wish. Period. Much more efficient than donating goods because transport would be rendered unnecessary as would armies of bureaucrats.

I found the idea attractive but I'm certain there must something wrong with it. Maybe it's that it smells of socialism and as such would never fly in the US. Or perhaps I don't trust ordinary people and am afraid that they would use the money to purchase nonsense and would end their lives happily starving.

The episode: After lunch and a nap, I strolled down a remote, bumpy dirt road for a hundred yards or so from where we are staying. Tethered cows munched contentedly in the fields, rice grew high, grey-green mountains framed the horizon. People greeted me as I ambled along. "Hello, Mister. How are you? Good afternoon. Where are you from?" I got into many amiable conversations. There was some begging but it was light and good natured.

I took many pictures again, mostly of the scenery.

A young woman with a little girl at her side stopped me. "My house collapsed," she said. "Do you want to see how we must live?"

She led me behind a couple of tents, one white and the other blue. She pointed to the few rocks scattered on the ground. "This is where my house once was," she said. Meanwhile the little girl, Manushka, age five, clutched my leg and looked at me, smiling in the most endearing manner.

The mother, whose name was Miriam, continued. "I am twenty-four years old. I have another child, a son, who is ten. He and Manushka go to a Christian school. I must pay for that. Our tent"—she pointed to the white tent behind us—"is hot both day and night. When it rains, the floor turns to mud. I barely have enough money to buy food."

I noted that Manushka had a protruding belly button, one of many signs of malnutrition.

Manushka was so incredibly cute—her grins, her pigtails, her insistence on hugging my leg—that I found myself saying, "I have a nice present for you, Manushka. It is in my room at Mon Petit Village. Wait here and I will bring it to you in a few minutes."

As soon as I said it I knew I had made a mistake. A harmless gift to one cute kid in a poverty-stricken country can cause a riot. But, once having promised, I persevered. I returned to my room and retrieved two Zutano-made toy rabbits. The second was a spare in case another child were to show up. I brought them back and gave one to Manushka. Sure enough, a three year old boy was visiting, perhaps a cousin.

"A girl rabbit for you, Manushka," I said. "And a boy rabbit for you," I said to the little boy whose name did not stay in my head long enough to report. Both children, were of course delighted.

"But let's keep this a secret between us," I suggested. "These are all I have."

Manushka, dancing up and down excitedly, waved goodbye as I walked back down the road to Mon Petit Village.

Monday, October 11. Morning. 6:20AM

There was a Voudon show here last night. It was not offered as a religious ceremony but rather as a show, a first rate performance including music, dance and the drawing of a complex *"veve"*—sacred symbols drawn in corn meal on the ground. A genuine Voudon ceremony would have been secret, not open to outsiders except under very special circumstances. In this case, seven American women attended who had arrived in the afternoon. Most were students from Duke university. They were here as volunteers through some Christian organization. Their task was to be useful in the area of maternal and child health. A few were university and charity staff members. The ceremony was in their honor.

The drumming, the singing and the dancing were at a very high level. There was little illumination thus rendering photography impossible but I did record the music on my iPod. I think one can get a good sense of the event by listening to it.

The volunteers have been collecting stories from survivors of the earthquake. They are impressed with the resilience of the Haitian people. I am, too. It may be felt by attending a folklore event like the one last night. The music and dance suggested an extraordinarily complex yet powerfully unified community. Each voice can be heard, some occasionally rising above the rest, but the threads come together to create a single, multi-tonal fabric. It is the same with dance. Each person does his or her own step but the steps come together and interact with one another and present an occasionally ferocious, almost military fabric continually interwoven with witty variations. The relation to jazz is obvious; palpable.

This is surely at once the most communal culture imaginable yet at the same time it comes across to us naively as utterly chaotic. The two extremes exist in the same space and time thus rendering Haiti impossible for the foreigner, me in this instance, to comprehend.

Haitians often seem unable to make sense of it either. In conversation with Jocelyn the other day she exclaimed that "this country needs a dictator." What a remarkable thing to say, I thought. And this from such a democratically inclined, well-informed person. The remark was made in the context of a discussion about a British group that was here to organize quake survivor camps.

"Why are foreigners needed to organize the camps anyway?" I asked. "Surely, Haitians are capable of organizing camps themselves and probably more effectively."

"Haitians are *incapable* of organizing themselves," Jocelyn said. "They are too competitive. Each person is out for himself."

Yet another conversation with this well informed, well intentioned person who proudly advertises the unity of the Haitian people.

This contradiction may also be seen in the international volunteers. There is a temptation to separate one's self from the NGOs—which are faulted certainly, faulted or worse—and to go it on one's own, developing projects here and there; being useful where one can in tiny venues. I am like that or was. David, the fellow with whom we talked yesterday, seems in that position which has the advantage of keeping one's nose to the ground. But the downside is that it adds up to very little. Nothing remains on the departure of the foreign initiator and besides, the scale is so tiny as to make no difference to the community—to say nothing of the country—as a whole.

Better, I think, to work with the best and largest organization one can find and use one's training and insights to create something programmatic and effective on a large scale; something related to the communitarian side of the Haitian culture but at the same time capable of satisfying the needs of the individual in a manner unlikely to end in mere selfishness.

We have the same problem in our own country. But in Haiti it is exacerbated to a frightening extreme. At times I worry that what we see in Haiti is a foretaste of America's future given the route we now seem to be taking. The only difference is that we do not have the positive side, an equivalent communitarian tradition.

October 11, 2010. Afternoon

My life here is routine. In the morning after breakfast I go off on an adventure, come back for lunch and spend the afternoon first with a nap and then the second shower of the day, insensitive perhaps given the uncertainty of the water supply but that is an understandable lapse, a privilege of the white skin if we must call it that. I get very hot—as does everyone here. I take a normal shower in the morning. No harm in that, I suppose, but I later permit myself the obscene luxury of a second one in mid afternoon.

Unfortunately, it is now almost two o'clock and our lunch has not yet been put out for us. Probably it is because the Duke University crew has gone and there is no food left in the house. Hunger, I suppose, gives me an unparalleled opportunity to experience solidarity with Haitians but, frankly, I get no pleasure out of it.

I hiked to town this morning once more and spent my time observing in the relatively progressive NEGES elementary school that is currently housed in tents in the back yard of the blue building that was its pre-earthquake home. This experience fit seamlessly with last night's Voudon show and the subsequent discussions we had about "the Haitian character" and how to help Haiti get its act together.

Now it all makes sense.

The answer is school. School is responsible for the ills we find here in this beautiful but traumatized country. No question about it. School is the culprit even more so than the earthquake. But it may also be Haiti's salvation.

I am not kidding.

Let me put it this way: This particular school probably constitutes the best of what is offered to children of the Haitian poor. It was founded by educators critical of slave-era French colonial schools in favor of ideas from such as Maria Montessori and Howard Gardner. John Dewey, too; their ideas have influenced the founding educators, Mme Yoleine Gateau-Esposito and James Filemy, both Haitian, now naturalized Americans working in US schools but spending considerable time each year back in Haiti to establish a plethora of imaginative programs. They are remarkable people. They offer schools that provide young Haitians the tools needed to make a difference.

So we see in these classrooms, children, unlike those in traditional Haitian schools, working at tables and sitting on chairs that are not fixed in place. Although they wear uniforms, there is a refreshing informality to the place—at least on the surface.

But I say there is much design work yet to be done. It is in the actual operation of the classroom that problems becomes apparent. The pedagogy remains a holdover from colonial education.

The children sit as passive recipients of material presented in a language that they don't understand. Their own language is Creole but instruction is in French—which is to a point defensible. Children anywhere need to be in command of an international tongue. But it strikes me that, despite the evident kindliness and compassion of the teachers, compelling methodologies have not yet been developed. In one classroom for the smallest children, two young teachers strolled from child to child repeating over and over and over again—in French: "How nice it is to be in school."

They must have said it at least a thousand times. Eyelids grew heavy, heads nodded.

In another classroom—one for older children—a textbook chapter covered the conquest of the Americas by the Europeans. What an opportunity for a classroom discussion! There was none.

In yet another classroom children were obliged to sing a song in four-four time. What a pity, I thought, that the music curriculum does not draw on the the complex, mellifluent tones and hypnogogic beats that we heard last night when the spirits were called.

All around us was plastic: plastic cups and dishes for lunch, plastic toys contributed by Americans, plastic dolls and plastic guns. And canned spaghetti for lunch. The possibility of US profit lurked everywhere not far beneath every surface.

The spark and intelligence to which we were exposed the previous evening were a universe away.

What if schools opened their doors to Haitian history and art? To Haitian folklore? To Voudon? What if children sang their own songs and wrote their own poetry and what if their own experiences and imaginations were central to the curriculum?

If such things were to be, Haiti might rise again.

Proposal: A teacher-training institute in Haiti in collaboration with an outstanding college of education. Bank Street comes to mind. There are others. The goal: To bring progressive education to Haiti, a project in concert with enlightened schools of education and universities anywhere in the world.

Our lunch has arrived!

Tuesday, October 12, 2010

Edy, the all-around handy fellow who has fixed the failing generator every night and then gets the wireless internet connection working, is also the owner of a large, serviceable station wagon and is known locally as a world-class chauffeur.

I hired Edy to transport Molly and me to La Vallée—"Lavale"— as it is spelled in Creole. The journey from Leogane to Lavale cannot be much more than thirty miles but it took us almost three hours. The mountains we crossed were high, the curves precipitous and, once we turned off the main highway at Carrefour St. Antoine and forded the river to make our way along the rutted and rock-strewn Lavale road, progress was very slow indeed.

Frankly, the thought of spending the night at CODEHA headquarters as I had perhaps a dozen times in the past did not appeal to me. I am too old now. Sleeping on a bulging mattress, sharing a room with someone who snores or who must put up with my snoring, having to use an outhouse crawling with huge insects, washing myself with water in a pan collected from the rain, all of this struck me as worthy and even enlightening but more suited to someone of Molly's age than mine. She is twenty. I am in my eightieth year. Besides, I rationalized, one of the many plans floating in my head is someday, perhaps soon, to organize a visit here of retirees from Kendal or elsewhere to see Lavale in all its glory, participate in some of its activities, and perhaps be motivated to become financial angels. And then, of course, to meet the legendary Gody, CODEHA's founder/director. It would therefore make sense to find appropriate quarters for people of my own cranky stage of life.

I had remembered that Gody once took me to have a look at the Prag Hotel in Tuff, the settlement of Ridore directly up the mountainside from CODEHA's headquarters. Lavale, more a township than a town, covers a large area comprising, I believe, fourteen settlements.

I checked into the Prag. Molly, Edy and I were served a basic spaghetti lunch there, hardly an elegant place but certainly adequate in that it has running water, real toilets—public—rooms that can be locked, and tolerably comfortable beds. There are no screens but bugs are few up here in the mountains although a small lizard raced cheerfully down my wall and scampered across my floor. There is only one other guest here and it will be me alone for dinner tonight.

On finishing lunch, Edy returned to Leogane while Molly and I hiked down the mountain to CODEHA headquarters. School children in neat blue uniforms returning home from their morning sessions raced past us with the speed and certainty of mountain goats, giggling in our direction perhaps because we were slow, white and foreign. But there were also a batch of warm-hearted young girls who walked thoughtfully beside us and, uninvited, reached for and held our hands. They redirected us when we missed the turnoff to CODEHA.

"CODEHA," Corde d'Enfants Haitianne, by the way, is a Haitian acronym meaning "Rope of Haitian Children," the idea being that alone we are a single thread. Together, we are a strong rope capable of hauling everybody up together.

We arrived at CODEHA and the almost adjacent community center to find everything deserted and locked. One guy was around, Jean Paul, a volunteer from the community who explained that 'Ti Ma, a long time stalwart of the organization, was off showing somebody a good place to go hang-gliding and would shortly return. He also said that a teacher, a certain Desiree, was in town and was expected soon.

We waited for what seemed like a long time. We were bored. I was concerned that Molly to whom I had presented CODEHA as a particularly exciting program, would be disappointed.

Then, a motorcycle came roaring up the very rough road. A man was driving behind whom was a large, cheerful woman—the long-awaited Desiree. She was actually more than a mere woman. She was a full-blown theatrical presence, a musical act of a memorable sort, a Mary Poppins as played by Ethel Merman. She talked loudly and fast, punctuating her sentences with raucous laughter while covering vast distances with each word. She leaves her listener far behind, scrambling breathlessly to catch up.

Desiree is a Canadian of mixed ancestry. She has the light brown skin and curly hair of someone with African genes but she claims also to have an Ukrainian background. I wouldn't be surprised if she were also part Jewish. Actually, her mother, she later told me, is from Trinidad. Father is Irish. Desiree speaks English as if it were her first language but claims that her French is even better. She is also comfortable in Spanish.

Desiree has traveled in many countries on a shoestring and impulse. She landed in Haiti soon after meeting Mme Carolle, a supporter of Gody's in San Diego, who told her of the remarkable work he was doing in Lavale. It sounded right to her so she hopped a plane and here she is.

"So ... where are you from?" I asked.

"San Diego," she said.

"You look Californian," I said, thinking of Hollywood.

"What does a Californian look like?" she asked.

If Desiree impressed me so strongly, one can only imagine the effect she had on the quietly rebellious Molly. Awestruck, Molly listened and grinned. For an aspiring hippy, this was a mentor from heaven.

Desiree has lived in Lavale for five months during which she became fluent in Creole and had a major impact on the CODEHA program. She has been giving music lessons to children, has organized song feasts and dramatic performances. She has taken an active role in the agricultural activities and showed us with pride the section of the garden where bamboo has been planted. Bamboo has many uses. It is both strong and flexible. As such it can be used as a building material that can mitigate the effects of earthquakes. It grows as quickly as a grass but its roots are deep enough to prevent soil erosion, a long-time major problem in Haiti.

Desiree showed us a garden in which what appeared to be a leafy vegetable—the name of which I did not jot down and have forgotten—was planted. This species, too, has diverse uses. It can be eaten but it can also be ground into a powder and mixed with water to create a better version of concrete.

We reminisced about Gody with whom she has worked very closely. Gody, we agreed, is a great and inspiring man who could become president of Haiti if he wished to run. He is faulted only when it comes to finances, organization and perhaps a few other practical matters. Despite her free style, Desiree seems to have a business-like mind and, although she receives no salary, is concerned about the financing of CODEHA as well as its organizational structure.

I told her of my recommendation that CODEHA become a "development partner" of Fonkoze, the Haitian micro-lending bank, giving it the capability of offering US tax credits to donors. Going that route would be better, I said, than forming an American CODEHA equivalent. I offered two reasons. First, it would avoid the paper work and bureaucratic structuring required of tax-exempt organizations. Second, CODEHA could certainly benefit from an affiliation with the far better known Fonkoze thus potentially attracting likely donors.

Beneath her *whoop-de-doo* Hollywood presentation Desiree is a cool, tough, business woman.

Desiree's way of thinking is a necessary corrective to the mental destruction of the Haitian young that has been accomplished by conventional schools. In such places as Haiti children are taught that there is only one right answer to everything; only one way to go about accomplishing anything. All one requires is a formula, a map, an instruction book which is to be memorized through deadening repetition. The end point is that the person becomes Zombified, trained to obey the orders of those in command.

Voudon represents the opposite, the imagination of the person within the womb, the soul of the culture, the socialized longing, the sensuality, the humor, the dizzying leaps of faith.

Gody, Desiree, indeed CODEHA, offer the children of Lavale the very soul of Haiti as well as a door to the larger world. And, hopefully, the gift to the world of Haitian culture.

October 13, 2010

"Time, as they say, flies." A. Chekhov.

I have only one more day in Lavale. On Friday Edy will drive me to Port-au-Prince and on Saturday I fly to New York.

Then on Sunday, I take a bus to Hanover to the Geezer Ghetto where Mary and I are now living. I am ready. I have enjoyed my time in Haiti as much as always but am frustrated that in the face of so many problems and so much readily available talent, little happens to alleviate the misery. In many ways things seem to be getting worse.

After a good night's sleep, an invigorating cold shower and a so-so breakfast consisting of a spicy omelette, canned orange juice, banana fritters, and all the white bread rolls one could eat, I hiked down the hill to CODEHA headquarters. It is very steep and maybe a mile long. It had rained last night and the yellow clay path has turned slippery. I picked my way down very carefully while carrying a large bag over my shoulder filled with gifts for CODEHA including a one-person tent, Zutano (my son's—Michael's—business) clothes and dolls, an old but working cassette recorder, and a couple of small books that I had self-published about Haiti one of which has a Creole text.

Lithe Haitians, children, farmers, and mothers trotted by me down the mountain quite effortlessly, all of them wishing me a cheerful good morning and a few offering to help carry my bag. But no. I was okay. I did slip a few times but never fell.

And there, more than fifty yards from the CODEHA community center, stood 'Ti Ma, machete in hand. We embraced, exclaimed how happy we were to see each other and inquired about each other's wives and children. 'Ti Ma is a great man. He is modest, laconic in a rural sort of way reminiscent of Vermonters I know. When he has something to say, it invariably has substance. He is profoundly loyal to his community, the Tuff settlement of Lavale, and works ceaselessly for the betterment of all its citizens.

'Ti Ma led me to where he and his family are now living. It is a meager, cluttered shack just across the path from the remnants of the concrete house that they had occupied until the earthquake destroyed all but part of its shell. Fortunately, no one was hurt.

This is a house that 'Ti Ma built with his own hands. Supplies had been purchased thanks to contributions from Vermont. It was one of several monuments to the spirit of solidarity between our state and Lavale, the other being the community center that has become an important focus of CODEHA and all of its programs and events.

'Ti Ma assured me that he will rebuild the house. It was one of the few that were destroyed in Lavale. Lavale survived the earthquake far better than the cities of Port-au-Prince and Leogane.

Mme Bertha, 'Ti Ma's wife, and I greeted each other with great warmth. They now have four children, three boys and a girl. The youngest, a thirteen month old boy, was on the floor in his baby chair, observing us. The next elder, a girl, age three, is in pre-school and the two older boys, seven and eleven are in elementary school. Education for these children was possible only because of a contribution made by an American man, a former volunteer, who took an interest in the family.

I laid out the gifts that I had brought, some for CODEHA and some for the family. The former was basically a tent, a simple one-person affair, that might be offered to visitors, I explained. I suggested that Molly might be the first to try it out tonight. I also gave the cassette recorder to CODEHA but preferably in 'Ti Ma's care. He said at once that he would use it to interview children and get down their stories.

'Ti Ma then uncharacteristically complained of his current financial problems. He works essentially full time for the community, for CODEHA. And not for money. He is a volunteer. He is an expert farmer, generous with his time and skills. The food he produces and everything at his disposal is given to the community. His friends and neighbors are more than generous with him in return. But that is not enough. The cash economy makes inevitable demands on him. Not everything can be grown through one's own efforts even when those of one's neighbors are added. There are certain foods one must buy in the market. 'Ti Ma takes responsibility for a community motorcycle that must be registered and insured. Clothes must be purchased. Gody has for years promised him that when it becomes possible, he will put 'Ti Ma on salary. But that time has not yet arrived and it may not ever.

It is not Gody's fault. He has no money either. The international community is to blame, the hundreds of NGOs in Port-au-Prince and the US, Canadian and French governments that promised the humanitarian assistance that never came.

"This is not a good situation," I said. "You should be earning enough money to lead a good life. We must find a way to raise funds for CODEHA salaries so that people without resources will not be limited to volunteering, many of them like you on a full-time basis. There must be a way of bringing this about."

Shortly after this conversation I ran into Desiree in the CODEHA yard and we engaged in a long discussion about funding. She agreed that lack of money is a huge problem. But neither of us had any good ideas on what to do about it.

The next event of the day was sky diving. Simon, a French sportsman currently living in the Dominican Republic, is an accomplished sky diver. He has been visiting Lavale for some time looking for a site for a sky diving business. Today he gave a demonstration to the community. A couple of hundred people arrived in a great field that looks over a particularly spectacular part of the valley. Simon unfurled his parachute and gave two glorious rides. The first was to 'Ti Ma and the second was to Desiree. The sun shone brightly and the wind was strong but not dangerous. The conditions were perfect. The crowds cheered when each of them was carried aloft and again when they landed.

Imagine Lavale becoming the center of a sport like that! Imagine the tourist business! Imagine the river of dollars! Imagine ....

This evening at the hotel I was unwinding from an exhausting day, eating my supper of goat meat, rice and beans, and banana fritters when I heard the mumble of a motorcycle engine in the yard. "They have come for me," I thought.

Sure enough in walked 'Ti Ma with another man, M. Toussaint, whom he introduced as the new "*gérant résponsable*"—manager—of CODEHA. His duties are unclear to me. But the four of us continued the discussions about money and organization that seems to have been the theme of the day. Although CODEHA is doing better than ever, its needs are increasing and, without adequate funding, the toll on everyone concerned has become intolerable. It is not only 'Ti Ma who is having a hard time of it.

We briefly considered various possible funding schemes including the recruitment of groups of good willed, wealthy retirees to come to Lavale in order to gain an understanding of what is being done to transform the economy and how they might help. But that strategy, although it might be successful, would only work episodically. What is needed is a product or service that might find an international market and that stands a chance of bringing in a predictable and solid income.

Thunder and lightning were in the air and coming closer. We decided to continue our discussion until tomorrow at four in the afternoon when the new manager will be free. Perhaps Desiree and others will join us.

I must sleep … again ….

Good night.

Thursday, October 14: My Last Day in Lavale

It is funny how things happen in Lavale, maybe elsewhere in Haiti, too, including Port-au-Prince. Maybe that's the way of the world. Random encounters lead to interesting possibilities. You just run into people and something comes of it, good stuff as well as bad. Random encounters are the fuel of life.

I went to Western Union this morning to cash another hundred dollars and buy Gourdes. I think I am doing okay money-wise. The five hundred dollars that I brought along this time will probably get me through despite the luxury of hiring private cars to travel between cities, something I would never have thought of doing in the old days when I was young.

I sat for a moment on the steps of the Community Bank trying once again to figure out the money system here when a well dressed woman approached and asked where I am from. "The United States," I said. "But where exactly?" she persisted. "I have been to the United States several times and know something of its geography.".

She had visited Florida and New York, mostly Queens, but had never heard either of New Hampshire or Vermont. Her name is

Claudette Hilaire. She is the founder and director of a small women's organization based in Lavale's hospital. It is called "PROFASEH" an awkward French acronym that stands for a phrase approximating, "Promotion of Families and Women in Society in the South East of Haiti."

We did not have time to talk very much. She was on her way to open her office at the hospital. I accompanied her. I learned a bit about her and her work and came away from our encounter with the instinct that she was an important contact for future volunteer groups. I took her card and she took mine. Cards are very useful in Haiti—indeed in most countries.

Yesterday afternoon I met someone very close to my heart, almost a daughter. Narline, is a young woman I had known since she was thirteen. She is now twenty-seven. She ran up to me in the street and gave me a huge hug as I was talking with the CODEHA people. We were so happy to see each other! I had known her grandmother, "Gran' Rita," a cousin of Gody's, who died three years ago, a marvelous peasant woman who was a major presence in the community. Narline and her sisters, Enid and Marie-Michelle, lived with Gran' Rita and sometimes her brother, Makise, lived there, too. I felt very close to them all. They had an another brother and sister from other parts of Haiti who visited from time to time but I was only slightly acquainted with them.

Narline has graduated university in Port au Prince with a degree in education. I am confident that she has the makings of a terrific teacher but so far she has not been able to find a job. She scrapes by, dividing her time between Port-au-Prince and Lavale where she stays in Gran' Rita's old house. Maybe if we can get something going here, a training program in collaboration with a progressive US college of education, we can find a job for Narline.

As I made my way back down to the hotel after all that, I noticed how clean the street was, doubtless swept this morning by earnest young girls. The flowers along the way were in bloom and the valley below was edenic in its glory.

I thought of the second dream I had before making this trip, the one about Haiti being more than okay, still lovely, still promising. I thought, "that was a dream that foretells the future."

Back to Port au Prince; then ... home.
Friday, October 15, 2010

It is early morning. In an hour or so Edy, the guy who drove me from Leogane, will pick me up and drive me to Port-au-Prince. Tomorrow, Saturday, I will be on the afternoon plane to New York, spend one night there and on Sunday will board a bus to Hanover into the sweet, loving arms of Mary at our Geezer Ghetto, the benign old folks home where all our needs and wishes are amply satisfied.

Molly will join me as far as Leogane. She will probably return to Lavale after a few weeks where she plans to remain until May or perhaps for the rest of her life.

It has been a fine three days in this town—plus the additional seven in other great Haitian venues. I will miss all of it—especially the people—but now I must dematerialize.

'Ti Ma asked me when I plan on coming back. "I don't know," I said. "Maybe in a year or two or maybe never."

"Never?" he said, "Why never?"

"I am an old guy," I said.

Yesterday was another good one and a fitting end to the entire adventure. Desiree met me as we had agreed at the front of my hotel, Le Prag. She had Molly with her plus 'Ti Ma and M. Toussaint, the guy 'Ti Ma introduced to me the other night as the new manager of CODEHA, "*le gérant résponsable.*" Both were on motorcycles.

A lot of conversation followed, indeed a full day of conversation beginning as we made up our way to the "Sister's School," an elementary and secondary Catholic girls' institution where Desiree was to teach two classes in music, a felicitous development in this country because music education is not known to be part of the curriculum in any school.

Molly and I waited in the yard while Desiree talked with the principal, a smiling nun in an antique, blue and white habit.

The hundreds of girls were at recess. All were in uniform, blue skirt and white blouse in keeping with the Sister's clothing. Some were running here and there but most were memorizing lessons by repeating them out loud to themselves. This was clearly a traditional Haitian school.

Girls gathered shyly around us, staring and smiling uncertainly. "They probably have never seen a white woman before," Desiree suggested referring to Molly, "certainly not one with blond hair. Nor," she added, "an old white guy."

I grinned back at the kids, slapping palms with those who came close and poking an occasional little one in the nose. They were becoming more relaxed and curious. We were soon surrounded by a great throng, probably a hundred but for all I knew it may have been thousands.

It was time for Desiree's first class. Desiree, followed closely by Molly and a pack of high energy youngsters, made their way *en masse* to the classroom. I came next surrounded by giggling children of all sizes. Not all were girls. There were a few boys among them.

It was a large class, somewhere around forty children, each assigned a desk that was fixed in place. Even before everyone was seated, Desiree began. She is a great performer as well as someone who delights in carrying on a witty dialog with her audience. Banter and jokes come easily to her. She laughed freely and now and then broke into hearty guffaws. The children could not get enough of her. The more she said, the more *they* said; and the more they said, the more she laughed, and the more she laughed, the more she carried the children along with her. Yet she was strict in her own way. When two girls showed up to class ten minutes late, she greeted them with a song she made up on the spot. A rough English translation might be, "You are late! You are late! It is not good to be late!"

Almost at once everyone joined in, singing raucously and clapping. The two culprits were not offended. They sang and clapped along with everyone.

The subject for the day was a categorization of all the instruments that might be found in an orchestra—piano, violin, cello, horns, drums, and so on. The idea was to decide what list to put each in: wind, strings, percussion or brass. Each instrument was imitated by voice.

Desiree has the makings of a world class teacher but the exercise was a bit silly. A lot of instruments may be seen as fitting in more than one category. An accordion, for example, she convinced the kids to categorize as a percussion instrument but the sound is made by wind ... well, who really cares?

The main thing is that in a conventional Haitian Catholic girl's school she got the kids to become wonderfully alive, giving them her full attention and theirs to her and everyone loving every minute of it.

Then Desiree led another class, considerably larger than the first. This class drew to a wowser of a conclusion with children coming up to the front of the class, each singing her own song or telling a riddle. Desiree got a bunch of geeky, shy boys to beat drums by banging on their desks. The rhythms were convincingly Voudon—at least to my limited ear. Desiree joined them by slapping on her own desk while wiggling her body in a distinctly un-nunlike manner.

At the very grandest of the grand finale Molly did a break dance and I led everyone in the song, "Sweetly Sings the Donkey at the Break of Day." The kids really got off on the "He-haw, he-haw, he-haw, he-haw, he-haw." When school was let out they brayed donkey-like as they rushed down the halls.

Desiree, Molly, M. Toussaint, 'Ti Ma and I went to a restaurant for a beer and to consider what had happened. We agreed that the performance suggested many things that CODEHA could do, not merely to raise money—although that is certainly important—but to make a significant difference in Haitian education. Desiree is a treasure and putting her together with the immensely talented children around here is the formula for an unique version of liberation-education ... whatever that may mean.

Having been in the Sister's School, M. Toussaint suggested that we walk down the street to the Brother's School where he teaches. This is the one that the refugee children from Port-au-Prince have been attending since the earthquake. Local high schoolers worked with them initially in the community but soon the brothers opened their doors. It was a clean, conventional-seeming place but I was pleasantly surprised to see some children's art—very little actually—on the walls.

It was beginning to rain. Jackson, a young motorcycle *chauffeur extraordinaire*, 'Ti Ma and M. Toussaint drove us down the slippery mountain on the back of their machines to CODEHA headquarters for a fine dinner prepared by Madame Maggie Gabrielle, a local woman who loves to cook for CODEHA and is very good at it. We gave her the old "Hip Hip Hooray!" which she clearly appreciated. Simon, the French sky diver who is living in the Dominican Republic, joined us.

The dinner was supposed to have been the venue for more conversation about programs and fund raising but it turned into a farewell party for Molly and me. It was all very convivial. Molly is going back with me to Leogane tomorrow and then I will proceed to Port au Prince alone.

And that's where I am now in the same guest house where I was a week ago, the one that caters to Protestant missionary do-gooders.

I have been stand-offish. But I did meet a couple of teachers from Canada and a husband and wife team from Spain. The latter are with "Psychologists Beyond Borders." They have been working in tent cities not so much doing therapy as training social workers. That's cool, I thought. But I keep thinking about Haitian resilience which impresses me as exceptional. Who needs psychologists? Anthropologists might make more sense.

"Haitians are very resilient," the man psychologist said. "They got over the trauma of the earthquake in a month. There is no trauma in the population any more."

"And what statistics have *you* gathered about Haiti?" the woman psychologist asked me.

"None," I said. "I write stories. Mostly fiction."

XV

PS

I'm the Amtrak Vermonter. We just pulled out of Hartford, Connecticut. Another four and a half hours to White River Junction, Vermont, where Mary will meet me, then to dinner and home in our own sweet retirement community, our cozy Geezer Ghetto.

There are many thoughts about the visit to Haiti that are rattling around my head.

There was the time that Carla was driving me down the Delmas hill to Wall's Guest House. I suggested that we stop at St. Joseph's Home for Boys, the first orphanage I knew in Haiti. I had heard that it had been destroyed by the earthquake.

We turned right at Delmas 97 making our way past the piles of rubble that had been homes, indeed rather nice, middle class houses some of them. St. Joseph's Home for Boys was once a structure of four stories. Most of it was now flat to the ground. A small part of the first story remained.

It was sad to look on this destruction. I was flooded by memories, largely pleasant ones, but they were clouded by considerable distaste and confusion.

The founder and director of the place, Michael Geilenfeld, came to Haiti some thirty years ago as an American monk in an order affiliated with Mother Theresa's group. He began by working with boys of the street in a small, informal group, sleeping and eating together where they could.

Michael asked the order to allow him to buy a building and open an orphanage but Mother Theresa forbade him for reasons known only to her. He therefore went off on his own, raised the necessary funds and opened his orphanage anyway.

It was an odd sort of place from the start, enormously successful eventually and consistent with Michael's vision.

Its oddness lay in the fact that, although it was an orphanage, it was also a guest house that provided visitors with comfortable beds, clean rooms and good food—all at a reasonable price.

The boys were staff.

Michael himself was an affable host. Many visitors to Haiti stayed there, American, Canadian and European; scholars, journalists, missionaries, various do-gooders and people of all political persuasions.

It brought in funds that were used for running the enterprise.

Prayers were regular and frequent, morning and evening and at special times on holidays. Discussions of religious matters took place on a regular basis as well.

Michael, although by then a saintly fellow of sorts, also gathered and maintained an impressive collection of expensive Haitian art that adorned the walls. Sometimes the orphanage felt more like a museum than a home. But the boys did keep a parrot and a dog and Michael employed a fine cook who is currently working for Carla.

St. Joseph's grew to become a cultural mecca, far from the hand-to-mouth days from whence it arose.

The boys were loyal to Michael and appreciated what he had done for them.

The building was huge by Haitian standards but did not house a large population, maybe thirty boys at a time. All went to school in the community and were also given an opportunity to take ballet and Haitian folk dance lessons. Some became quite accomplished at this. The troupe made regular tours of the US midwest where Michael was from. The boys raised money in the process and in so doing added to their sense of self worth and the apparent affluence of the orpanage.

Michael expanded the edifice. Every few years a new story was added. When I last visited several years ago, it had four. At the very summit was a chapel.

Michael also founded affiliate orphanages. One, still functioning despite reported earthquake damage, is "Wings of Hope." It is for handicapped children and is located in Fermath on the mountain above Petionville. Another is in the city of Jacmel. I do not know if it still stands. Both were run by graduates of St. Joseph's.

I admired what Michael was able to do even though his vision was different in many respects from my own. But at the same time, there were some things about him that bothered me. His religion, studiously pious, rang with Hallmark card, holier-than-thou, sentimentality.

However, what made me far more uncomfortable had to do with human relations. It was hard to put my finger on. There were often, for example, older, white women around, mothering types, who seemed to worship Michael, outdoing one another in being helpful.

And then there was an occasional, young adult Haitian guy hanging around who did not seem to be affiliated with the place. One of these in particular struck me as flambouyantly sexual in appearance and manner.

I never knew Michael to be in an obvious love relationship with a woman or a man. Nonetheless, St. Joseph's seemed, in its way, a very sexy place.

It sometimes occurred to me that Michael was gay. But so what?

Businesslike but informal, that was Michael's style. While helpful to the boys in the sense of feeding, housing and educating them, he seemed personally almost stand-offish. He was generous but not exactly warm, compelling in his manner rather than intrusively demanding. If I were asked, I would have called him an amiable social loner, a thoughtful host and a good businessman.

But then came the accusations and the publicity. On a dance tour to the American midwest in the early '90s, several of Michael's boys asked for and received asylum on the grounds that he had allegedly abused them sexually. The news hit the papers both in Detroit and Port-au-Prince. Some years later another group of boys made a similar claim but were denied asylum. Haitian social services investigated Michael and did nothing, presumably giving him a clean bill of health.

The word on the street about Michael became very bad. People claimed to know for sure that he was a sexual predator, stories were told but hard data was hard to come by. Michael denied everything. He insisted that the appeals for asylum that we heard about were a function of the attractiveness of America's wealth to poor boys from the streets.

Some Haiti-based US Catholic clergy stayed clear of him. He was not part of their circle. One nun I ran into was particularly harsh in her criticism. She believed the rumors. A respected orphanage director believed them, too.

I interviewed some of oldest and most articulate of Michael's boys. A representative answer: "He never bothered me. I don't know what he may have done to other kids but whatever might have been bad was not as important and the good he did. If not for him I would have been dead on the streets a long time ago."

About ten years ago I decided I that could not stay at St. Joseph's Home for Boys again and remain above suspicion in my own work with children. I thought it was best to explain this to Michael. He was very angry. We have not spoken or written in about four years.

I was sad to see the earthquake's utter destruction of the house. None of the boys were hurt and that is a "blessing" as Michael would say. Would he also say that the destruction was God's work?

Carla drove her car too close to what remained of the building. Her front and rear wheels both climbed the curb. I thought that we were stuck for good. But eight young men were watching us, neighborhood guys just hanging out. They were not part of the orphanage. But they knew Carla and liked her. All of them together pushed and shoved and after no more than ten minutes they had us on the road again.

That was typical of Haiti at its best—and Vermont, too—no one asked for nor expected anything in return. This was an act of friendship and responsibility. It was what anybody would do.

We take care of each other.

What remains of all this? Nothing. Worlds have faded to mist. All that is left are bursts of light chasing shadows on a shimmering screen that rolls up like a window shade. Glories are ephemeral, twilight images and ill- remembered anecdotes, tales of what might have been, dreams, fairy tales of altruism on behalf of sad and beautiful children.

Gordie? I see him still in my mind's eye. He was the red headed ten year old blind kid who heedlessly loped down the hill at the New Jersey Camp for Blind Children yelling, *"Outta my way, everybody! Blinker coming!"* ["Blinker": blind-kid slang for "blind kid."]

He is probably seventy-something years old now.

And I can see those three boys, children of the streets, who sleep on the trampled grass of Chanmas, the central park of Port-au-Prince. "Where are you staying, Mister, which hotel?"

"Saint Joseph's Home for Boys," I said

"An orphanage, ain't it?"

"Yes."

"Can you get us in there?"

Bob's Bio

I grew up in New York's Greenwich Village during the frothy 1930s and 1940s.

My family, never far from its Russian roots, was, like that of most of my friends, artistically inclined, secular Jewish, and politically on the humanistic left.

Before my birth, my father was a consultant to the Soviet Jewish land settlement movement.

My mother had been a preschool teacher trained in the Dewey tradition. I was therefore destined to experience several remarkable progressive schools including Bank Street kindergarten, City and Country School, the Little Red Schoolhouse and the Elisabeth Irwin High School.

Then came a conventional interlude at Cornell University. I received a Ph.D. in Clinical Psychology from Columbia's Teachers College, a return to the Deweyan world.

Given this upbringing, it is hardly surprising that my career has concerned children in summer camps, schools, communities and institutions.

For fifteen years my office was in a Vermont forest where kids and parents would come for a day or so to think through personal or family issues.

On retirement in 1995, I began annual visits to Haiti and Russia where I got to know young people surviving without family help.

I have written several books and have taught at Harvard, Boston College, Boston University and Concordia University. I was the founding dean of Goddard College's individualized master's degree program.

My wife, Mary, is a well-known feminist scholar; co-author of "Women's Ways of Knowing." We now live in Kendal at Hanover, a very nice, Quakerish retirement community, our sweet Geezer Ghetto.